Talking to the Dead

Talking to the Dead

Alison Morgan

Magpie Books

Constable & Robinson Ltd
3 The Lanchesters
162 Fulham Palace Road
London W6 9ER

www.constablerobinson.com

This edition published by Magpie Books,
an imprint of Constable & Robinson Ltd 2010

A copy of the British Library Cataloguing in
Publication Data is available from the British Library

ISBN 978-1-84901-549-3

Printed and bound in the EU

1 3 5 7 9 10 8 6 4 2

Contents

Introduction: Talking to the Dead

When a loved one dies, people often feel that their relationship with them and their communication with them are unfinished. Many of the stories in this book relate their disbelief or inability to accept that someone they were close to has passed away and is gone forever. The belief in an afterlife remains strong and finding a way to communicate with people who have passed away has preoccupied mankind throughout history and across many continents.

Acknowledged reports of clairvoyants span centuries and cultures. There have always been some who claim to have had a communication from a deceased loved one and others who believe that they have the 'gift' of being able to stay in contact with all spirits from the afterlife.

Stories of communicating with the dead have been in

circulation since early human existence. The Old Testament tells the story of the raising of the spirit of the dead prophet Samuel so that the Hebrew king Saul could question him about a forthcoming war. Ancient Hindu scrolls dating back to the twelfth century tell of how clairvoyance is one of the siddhis (accomplishments) that may be gained through meditation and discipline.

In a similar way some branches of Tantric Buddhism also hold the belief that communion with the dead can be reached through self-discipline and meditation. The Lakota Sioux believe that the human soul is intertwined with the life force of everything in nature and that each force has its own unique spirit, not just people, but animals, trees, rivers, and even mountains. This life spirit, or Niyan (breath of life), lives on long after the body dies. At the moment of death, the Niyan passes into another level of existence, 'the shadow world', or as we would call it, the afterlife. The Sioux have always also believed that some individuals can communicate with the dead, locating and helping lost souls or healing the ailing spirits of the living.

Many people who report an experience of communication with a deceased person are in childhood or young adulthood. Some believe that this is because children and young adults are more susceptible to the spiritual realm. (In fact, current thinking in clairvoyant circles holds that most of us are born with clairvoyant abilities but then start to turn them off as we are brought up to become sensible adults, able to adhere to demonstrable social norms).

Introduction

Some stories of communication with the dead are associated with religious figures and saints but are more likely to be about deceased relatives and friends. Many people have stories about how they knew instantly when a loved one died even though they were not with them at the time. There are also stories about how a deceased loved one helped or warned them when they were in danger or comforted them when they felt down.

To most of us, the most familiar way of contacting the dead is through a medium, sometimes called a psychic or spiritualist. A medium is someone who believes they can listen to and relay messages from the spirit world meant for people here on Earth.

Some claim to be able to speak directly with the spirit, allowing the spirit to literally speak through them by using their voice. Others report that they are able to gain information about a loved one who has passed away by holding something that once belonged to the deceased person. This type of clairvoyance is sometimes called physical mediumship and may involve perceptible manifestations, such as loud raps and noises, voices, materialized objects including automatic writing, materialized spirit bodies, or body parts such as hands, and levitation.

The medium is used as a source of power for such spirit manifestations. Many people also claim to be able to communicate with spirits through electrical equipment and radio waves emitting from televisions, telephones and computers, detecting types of energy not normally perceptible to humans.

Introduction

The understanding of modern medium psychic ability or spiritualism dates back to the mid-nineteenth century when the religion of Spiritualism was formed in the United States of America and the United Kingdom.

In his book *The Spirits Book* (1860), Allan Kardec lists five ways of communicating with spirits: Clairvoyance, where someone can see things that are not physically present or see and understand things through inanimate objects belonging to a deceased person; Clairaudience, when someone can hear the voices of spirits; Clairsentience, the ability to sense that a spirit is present; Claircognizance, knowing that something life-changing has happened or is about to happen, such as someone's death or birth; and Clairalience, the ability to smell a spirit, usually in the form of perfume or tobacco.

Many mediums now believe that they have what they call a spirit guide, a spirit who aids the medium with developing their abilities to communicate with the dead and sometimes brings the spirits to them so that they can talk. Others argue that they can talk with spirits directly without the need for a spirit guide of any kind.

Although there are many sceptics and doubters, the widespread belief in and recorded experiences of clairvoyance and psychic abilities have prompted many world governments, including the US and the former Soviet Union, to fund and undertake scientific research into the subject. In the US, the Society for Psychical Research has been undertaking research into paranormal and clairvoyant abilities since the 1970s.

Introduction

In 1972 in a connected study with the SPR, Harold Puthoff and Russell Targ conducted research into whether individuals claiming to have psychic powers could correctly identify something that they couldn't see, using only their minds. This study at the Stanford Research Institute concluded that 'remote viewing' a term coined by Targ and Puthoof, was and is possible. They believed that many famous practitioners of psychic ability, such as Uri Geller, Pat Price and Ingo Swann, had what could be described as extra sensory psychic abilities.

Of course there are those who question this theory, most notably psychologists David Marks and Richard Kammann, authors of *The Psychology of the Psychic* (1980). However, it would seem that rather than psychic ability being considered to be merely the hocus-pocus of the Victorian fairground, many scientists do believe that we may have powers of the mind as yet not fully understood

Whatever your viewpoint on the subject, one cannot deny that the whole topic of paranormal experiences is intriguing and compelling. The accounts in this book have been collected from many different people, of varying ages, cultures and lifestyles. In some cases the respondents asked me to change names, places and other details so that they couldn't be identified. All are convinced that they have had contact with the spirit world. They have had loved relatives say farewell as they pass away, spirits helping them or even saving them in times of difficulty and, in some cases, the spirits of the departed who they never met coming back for a visit.

Introduction

Beware though, not all of these accounts are heart-warming tales. There are those who have attempted to contact the spirit world with scary results. As I have noted, this is an area of which, as yet, we have a limited knowledge, and until we do we must be careful in our expectations of it. However, in the end the fascination in reading these accounts of people's experiences of talking to the dead lies in the fact that they cover such a wide variety of situations and personalities.

Final Goodbyes and Reassurance

*Coming to terms with the death of a loved one
and moving on.*

When someone we love dies, it's often hard to come to terms with our loss. People often react with disbelief, and have the feeling that they are unable to move on without that person in their life.

Many of the accounts in this section are heart-warming tales of the farewells of loved ones as they pass into the afterlife. They concern messages from the dear departed, encouraging those left behind to carry on as well as stories offering evidence that our loved ones can still take care of us – even from beyond the grave.

Harriet, 75

My husband of forty years passed away a few years ago and I grieved for him so much that I eventually decided to sell the house we had shared because it held too many memories and I thought I needed to move on. I viewed many houses and eventually decided to buy one that I had fallen in love with.

Boxing up the belongings in our house was quite traumatic as it felt as if each piece held so many memories. When the final items were ready to move and had been taken away by the removal men, I sat in the empty house and cried thinking of all the happy times I had had there with my husband.

After I had finished crying I felt a strange warm glow around me and felt something I can only describe as relief. I got into my car and drove to my new house and when I opened the door I felt the glow again. Some time later I went to see a medium with my sister and even though I am usually sceptical of these things the experience was astonishing.

The medium told me that she had a message for me from David (my husband's name). He was glad that I had moved and wanted me to be happy in my new house. She told me that he still loved me and knew that I loved him but that he didn't want me to be unhappy and living in the past. The warm glow I had felt during moving house was him supporting my decision. I don't usually believe that mediums can contact the dead but I have to say that in my case it was a heart-warming and moving experience.

James, 46

At Christmas time, around three years after my mum died, my wife and I were visiting my father's home. My parent's house has a beautiful real fireplace and, as it was cold, dad had a blazing fire going.

As we were sitting watching television, our eyes were drawn to a shape being formed by the flames. The shape looked exactly like the Christmas flower arrangement that my mum used to make to decorate the house.

The flames then seemed to change shape and all of us were convinced that they turned into an image of my mothers face. She was smiling as if she was happy to see the family all together and my dad told me that he often saw her face smiling at him and that he believed that it was her way of telling him not to be sad and that they would be together again one day.

Cathy, 39

My son Joe drowned when he was just seven years old and I have never got over his passing.

One day I was walking in the countryside miles from anywhere when my thoughts returned to him and my grief once again made me feel crippled with exhaustion. I asked Joe to give me a sign that he was still with me and that I hadn't lost him forever.

I suddenly heard a voice telling me to go to the village. I didn't even know there was a village there, but as I walked on I did come across a tiny village with a little teashop. I went into the teashop to recover from my walk and my exhausted grief.

The shop was selling home made cherry pie which had been Joe's favourite and as I ordered it tears came to my eyes knowing that this was the sign that his spirit was still with me.

Colleen, 50

In the 1970s my older sister was murdered as she returned from a night out with her friends. She was 19 at the time and I was only 15. I was devastated to lose my big sister; she was someone who I had always looked up to. I used to borrow her clothes and experiment with her make-up. She never seemed to mind and she was always willing to give me a 'make-over'.

I got married in 1990 and as I was getting ready I began thinking about how I wished that my big sister was with me, helping me get ready and doing my hair. The next thing that happened was completely bizarre.

When I looked into the mirror it wasn't me I saw, it was my sister, looking just as she had when she was alive. She said to me that I wasn't to worry about her. She was alright and she told me that she was very happy that I was getting married and that she would be with me the whole day. I felt a lump in my throat and turned away from the mirror.

When I turned back she had gone and the reflection was of me again. I swear that the whole day I *could* feel that she was with me and my wedding day was perfect. I talk to her now because I do believe that she was listening.

Ella, 40

As a little girl I was always very close to my granddad. During school term time I spent every weekend at my grandparents house and my granddad would spend hours telling me stories of my mum as a little girl, things that he and my grandma had got up to when they were first married, him being one of nine brothers and his experiences looking after German prisoners of war during the Second World War.

When I had my dancing lessons on Saturday morning, granddad would walk me there and collect me later. He loved eating butter mints and the smell of mint combined with the smell of pipe tobacco always reminds me of him.

He passed away when I was twenty-six and I was devastated. It just seemed inconceivable to me that I would no longer hear his pretend grumbling at me when

I was doing something naughty (he used to growl like a bear if I was being annoying.)

He died suddenly after suffering a massive heart attack. I even bought a packet of butter mints and a pouch of pipe tobacco so that I could still smell him but it wasn't the same. But I still talk to him in my head every day and I hope that he is able to hear the things I say to him.

Felicity, 34

I was very close to my mom but when she died I was not present for her death and so longed to know that her sudden stroke had not been a terrifying event for her. I needed to know that she hadn't suffered. It came as such a shock that I just kept asking 'Why, why?'

Within weeks of her death I received my answer. I had a very vivid dream in which my mother took me to the scene of her stroke and as the scene happened I was able to comfort her. I then asked her why and she told me that she had been feeling tired but that she was always watching over me.

What she hadn't told the family was that she had also been diagnosed as having Alzheimer's disease and had been worrying that she would become a burden on the family. She told me that she was in a better place now and that she was happy. From when I awoke the next morning I felt more peaceful than I had for weeks. It felt like a great weight had been taken from my shoulders.

Megan, 73

In January, 1998, I returned home after a month in hospital in Oklahoma. I had had a heart attack and when I was first admitted to ER they weren't sure whether or not I'd survive. I had further problems in the hospital but with various treatments and medication I eventually began to get better.

When I arrived home I found a letter from my mom informing me that my cousin Stella had died suddenly in a car accident. I was so upset because Stella and I had always been close. However, just as I put the letter down the phone rang, when I answered it a familiar voice said 'Hi Megan, it's Stella.'

Furious that this was some kind of sick joke I immediately slammed the phone down. I was shaking; it was very upsetting to have to deal with that phone call just then. The phone rang again and the same voice asked after my health. The caller insisted she had been with me in the hospital, she even told me about treatments I had had when I knew that there were no visitors with me. It was creepy. The caller's voice wasn't too clear then it faded all together and there was just static.

The last thing I heard was, 'Megan I will call you again.' It sounded exactly like my cousin Stella but I was never sure if it could have been her from beyond the grave. She did appear to know things that had happened in the hospital that I don't know how she could have known. Maybe after she died she began to watch over me in the hospital to make sure that I got better.

Stacy, 24

My daughter Maisy died when she was just two years old. It was very difficult for me and because I'm sentimental in that way I have kept some of her favourite toys. One of her toys is a rabbit that talks if you touch it. Whenever I am sad the toy begins to make a noise as if someone has touched it. It only ever happens if I am sad or worried about something and I think it is my daughter trying to comfort me.

One night I was talking to my mum on the phone in my bedroom and I felt someone sit on the bed next to me. Not a heavy adult but light, like a child. I then felt something lean against my right side. I told my mum what was happening and I could hear her catch her breath. We both said at the same time, 'Maisy!' As I said her name I felt my right side where she was leaning get warm and I felt so comforted.

Now whenever I feel down I can feel her sleeping next to me as if she needs to tell me that she's OK. I feel that she is telling me to move on with my life.

Bill, 37

Sadly, my grandpa was diagnosed with stomach cancer in 2005. We were all very upset by the news but he survived quite well for a while on medication and hospital treatments. However, in early 2007 he took a turn for the worst and had to be hospitalised. We all took turns at visiting him and sitting by his bedside but he was barely conscious most of the time.

Our neighbour Glenda was a nurse and had often dropped by his house to check on him when he was at home while he was ill, and she also took turns at visiting him. My grandpa was very fond of her because she was such a caring person

He died at around 3.30 in the morning and my mum and grandma were with him to say goodbye. It was very upsetting because we loved him so much. When we went round to tell Glenda that he had passed she told us a funny thing happened during the night.

At about 3.30 or 4 o'clock she had woken up and gone downstairs to get a drink of water and had noticed a white mist out on her lawn. She said she then heard my grandpa's voice saying 'Bye'. After we told her that he had died she was convinced that he had stopped by to say his goodbyes to her because she had been so kind to him.

Kelly, 34

My father died two months ago, it was unexpected because he was only 55 years old and always very active. Many strange things have started to happen since his passing.

Lights have been flickering on and off, the TV keeps loosing its signal yet when the TV repair guy came round, he couldn't find anything wrong with it and our neighbours aren't having any electrical problems so it's not the local electricity company having problems.

One afternoon I was having a nap and awoke to hear my father's voice saying, 'goodbye sweetheart'. At the same time the car on our driveway beeped its horn. The car horn beeped again the other day and now I believe that it's my father telling me he's still looking out for me.

Rachel, 22

I lost my grandfather last Christmas. He died after having a massive stroke that caused severe brain damage. He never regained consciousness and spent the final days of his life in a coma. It happened so suddenly the whole family were in shock. The hospital telephoned our house at around 5.45am giving us the information that he had died, it was weird because I had been having a vivid dream about my granddad just before the telephone woke me up.

Immediately we began calling the rest of the family to tell them the sad news, before heading to the hospital. When we arrived at the hospital we were told that he had passed away at 5.30am. My mom works as an ER nurse and had been on duty the morning he died. She was told while she was at work and came to join us as soon as she could as we said our goodbyes to granddad.

The following morning, my grandmother came to stay with us. She told us that she was sure that my grandfather had died around 4am, not 5.30. My grandmother had apparently woken up at 4.30am on the day that he passed and had seen him in her bedroom wearing the same pyjamas that she had taken to the hospital shortly after he was admitted.

She was so startled by what she saw that she couldn't get back to sleep so she got up to make some coffee. When the call came from my mom, she was sitting at the kitchen table wondering what her vision could possibly mean. Mom and Dad just presumed that it was grandma half dreaming just before waking up and granddad had appeared in the dream.

Later that same day my aunt (my mom's sister), came round. As we all sat in the living room, she began to tell us how she had woken up at 4.30am and had heard her dad (my granddad), saying goodbye to her. When she looked around she couldn't see anyone.

She had presumed that she had simply been dreaming but when my grandma told her how she had woken up at the same time and had seen my grandfather in their bedroom we all thought that this was very strange. I had been dreaming about him as well.

My grandmother is convinced that he had come to say goodbye just before he died which is why she feels so sure that he had died by 4.30. Both my aunt and my grandmother woke at the same time. I was dreaming about him. My mom is a nurse and was awake but we're wondering now if she had been asleep would granddad have come to say goodbye to her too?

Katherine, 43

In March 1998, a man I was in a relationship with committed suicide. He was living in a house with my elderly uncle, Eddie and had been going through a terrible time financially. He shot himself with Eddie's gun, I was devastated. Eddie was 80 years old and not in particularly good health, and often spoke frankly with me about dying.

When he saw me at my boyfriend's funeral he told me that he felt that he was not long for this world and that when he died he would find my boyfriend and tell him that I was sorry that I had not been able to help him through that difficult time in his life that caused him to self-destruct.

Eddie died in June 1998. The following Christmas I was watching TV in my sitting room with a man I had just started dating when two figures appeared in the corner of the room. The figures were Eddie and my former boyfriend. I asked Jack, the man who was with me if he could see anything but he couldn't.

My former boyfriend was smiling and Eddie was nodding his head. I think they came back to tell me that it was OK that I had begun to move on.

Cecile, 20

In 2000, my great-grandmother died after a long illness. After the funeral, the family gathered at my great-grand-father's house for the wake. I remember my sister, who was seven at the time, sitting in the bedroom where my great-grandfather used to sleep. She was crying.

From where I stood in the bedroom doorway I suddenly saw my great-grandmother float down from the ceiling above the bed. She passed through the mattress then stopped between the floor and the bottom of the bed.

She wasn't on the floor - she was hovering a few inches above it, just floating in mid-air. She looked at my sister and said, 'I'm with Jesus now, Jodie. Don't worry about me' With that, she disappeared once again.

No one believes me when I tell this story but I know what I saw.

Adam, 48

My wife Norma lost her mother when she herself was in her early thirties. She still misses her very much. Last year, the night before her birthday, Norma couldn't sleep and so got up and sat in the living room to watch TV. That particular night she was feeling a bit sad at having another birthday without her mum being with her and thinking about the fact that her own children were nearly grown and would be going off to college soon. Eventually she felt ready to come back to bed.

The next morning, while preparing breakfast she was watching the TV in the kitchen when the cookery segment came on. The item was on cake decoration and they had made a birthday cake.

To my wife's surprise, when they showed the finished cake to the camera, the words, 'Happy Birthday Norma', were written on it. My wife took this as a sign from her mother to wish her a happy birthday. It was because she had felt sad in the night. Her mum wanted to cheer her up in the morning.

Barbara, 53

I was very close to my mom who sadly passed away two years ago. Whenever I needed help or guidance I would always turn to her and heed her advice. She died rather suddenly from the internal effects of a fall in our local shopping mall and the hospital called me at work to tell me that she had died. The last time I saw her had been the previous weekend when we'd enjoyed a barbecue because it had been such a lovely day.

I cried for months after she had passed and whenever I was faced with a tough decision I just didn't know what to do. In desperation I contacted a medium who came to do a reading in my house.

He told me that my mother was always with me and all I had to do was ask her to give me a sign whenever I needed some help.

Later that week, I was invited to apply for a promotion at work and didn't know if I should do so or try for another job somewhere else. I'd had a little difficulty with being bullied at the place where I then worked and my mom had always given me a sympathetic ear.

A promotion would mean that I was out of the way of the two bullies but still in the same company. I asked my mum to send a rainbow if I should apply for promotion or heavy rain if I shouldn't.

The next day it was pouring down when I woke up. I didn't apply for a promotion and during my lunch break went to see a job agency about finding a new job. Within a month I was working at my current employers where the staff are lovely and I'm so much happier.

Now I talk to my mom all the time. She sends me messages through bumper stickers, posters, music and radio. I feel so blessed not to have lost her completely.

Suzanne, 40

My grandmother was the most important person in my life. On the night she died I was sitting by her hospital bed. Although the tears were pouring down my face I held her and asked her to come back to me in any way she could. She was a lovely woman who I know for sure has gone to heaven because she looked after me so well. Before her death she had told me many times that she would never leave me and would be always watching me from heaven.

When I arrived home on the night she passed away, the telephone kept ringing. My grandmother would telephone me every week for a chat since we now lived in different cities. Many times I would come home to an answer phone with the message light flashing and I knew that the message would be my grandmother.

The phone rang at least ten different times that night, each time I answered it all I could hear was static crackling. The following day when I returned from work the answer phone was flashing. When I played back the messages they were the same as the previous nights, just static. I think it was my grandmother trying to reach me. Whenever I'm feeling down the phone rings and I hear the same crackling noise. If I'm out, there will be a message when I get home that is just the scratchy noise. It has to be my grandmother still letting me know that she is OK.

Sue, 33

When I was a teenager, I had a boyfriend called Ronnie. It was the stuff of teenage romance. He had the scruffy hair and biker jacket, the old car; the works. Eventually we broke up when we went our separate ways when he went to college but we stayed in touch and remained close friends.

About two years after I had broken up with Ronnie, I fell pregnant by the boyfriend I was with at the time. I was ecstatic, I had always wanted a baby. My boyfriend however, didn't like the news at all. He argued that I should get rid of it but I couldn't. In the end he left me and I went through with the pregnancy on my own.

Years earlier I had talked with Ronnie about babies and the future and he told me that he loved babies. His eldest sister had a baby girl when he was eighteen and he adored her. When I told Ronnie the news about my pregnancy he was delighted. The next time he visited he brought all kinds of baby things as presents and seemed really delighted that I was going to have a baby.

While pregnant, I began dating another man who is now my husband. He also loves children and was happy to bring up another man's child. I had a little girl who I called Cassie. Ronnie remained part of our lives and whenever he turned up to visit he always brought a present for Cassie. Needless to say she really looked forward to his visits and would run down the driveway shouting 'Ronnie! Ronnie's here'.

When my little girl was six, Ronnie died in a road accident. I was devastated and so was Cassie. He had been such a lovely man and a good friend to us both. About a week after the funeral I woke up hearing my daughter chattering with someone in her bedroom. Thinking that she was playing when she should be sleeping I poked my head around the door.

Cassie was sitting up I bed but not awake. She had that kind of glassy-eyed look that you get when you are sleep-walking. I distinctly heard her laugh and say 'No, Ronnie'. She seemed to be making some arrangements to take the dog for a walk with him, which she always loved to do.

The next morning at breakfast Cassie staring telling me that Ronnie talked to her at night and they made plans to walk the dog at the weekend. I didn't want to upset her so I just listened sympathetically.

The following Saturday, to my surprise, Ronnie's mum Glenda, brought her dog round to see if Cassie wanted to walk him with her. When they got back Cassie told me that Ronnie had been with them the whole way and said he would visit her again soon. I'm not sure if she really is communicating with Cassie or if it's her very vivid imagination but whatever it is, it has made her happier.

Julia, 29

My dad had been in hospital with terminal cancer for two weeks. Three weeks ago, at exactly 4 o'clock in the afternoon, I was writing a report for work when my computer crashed. Ten minutes later my brother called and told me that our father had died at 4 o'clock.

I immediately smelled a very flowery scent flowing through the room. When I arrived at the hospital, my sister had already arrived and she told me that her car had broken down at exactly 4 o'clock too. We believe that it was our dad calling for our attention as he passed away.

Griselda, 26

When I was around four years old and my brother was three, we lived in a small house with just our mother and grandma. Next door was a lady called Sue who lived with her son Jimmy. Our mother and Sue were friends and we often went over to visit. Jimmy was nearly ten years old but he enjoyed playing with us and we loved to visit him.

I remember going over there one spring with our mum. My brother and I decided to play outside because the weather was turning warm. We spent some time playing ball with Jimmy until one of his friends came to call for him and the two of them went off to do whatever bigger boys did. Once he had gone I began to explore the yard. Sue had a big shed behind her house that I had never been into. On that day however, I couldn't resist opening the day to have a peak inside.

The shed was filled up with old furniture from floor to ceiling. There was a small amount of space to walk along between the stacks of furniture and I crept inside.

Suddenly I saw a movement to my left and when I looked I saw an old lady drinking a cup of tea.

She wasn't scary but I couldn't understand why she wasn't in the house. She said she couldn't go in there any more now and that she would rather keep watch from where she was. She seemed very calm and happy and I chatted with her for a while. Then she told me it was time for her to go. She told me to tell everyone goodbye from her and got up and walked quietly outside. I ran to the door and looked out but she had gone.

Eventually my mother called for us to join her because it was time to go home. I told her about the old lady and that she had said to tell everybody goodbye but I think my mum thought that it was just my imagination.

Later that evening though, Sue came round seeming very upset about something. My mother went outside with her and they talked quietly for a while before both coming into the kitchen. Sue had just had word that her grandmother had died and she was devastated.

My mother made some tea and we all sat at the kitchen table. I told Sue about the old lady in her shed and she went pale. As I described her she told me that I was accurately describing her grandmother who I had never met. When I told her that the old lady was drinking tea she laughed.

Apparently, her grandmother had been addicted to tea and drank around twenty cups a day. I told Sue that the old lady had told me to say goodbye to everyone and Sue's eyes filled with tears again.

We were all sure that her grandmother had paid her a

last visit to say goodbye. Perhaps she had appeared to me not Sue because she didn't want to upset her.

Megan, 49

About five years ago, I awoke very early in the morning and felt as if someone was hugging me tightly in their arms. I had a sensation of such love and warmth flowing through me.

The whole sensation puzzled me and I got up for a while and had a cup of tea, wondering what was going on. The next day I was told that my son, who lived in California, had died at 5am. He had been in a car crash and the paramedics couldn't revive him. I now know that he dropped by to say goodbye before he passed to the other side.

Portia, 30

When I was at university, my grandmother lived with my mum and dad and my older sister. She had been suffering from arrhythmia of the heart and needed quite a bit of help getting out and about and doing things. My mum later told me that she had been unwell for a few days with a lack of appetite and weakness.

That night she called out for my mum in the night and when my mum went in to her she saw that my grandmother was having a heart-attack. My mum called for my older sister to get an ambulance and my grandmother was taken to hospital. They tried to revive her on the way but couldn't. My grandma was pronounced dead when she arrived at the hospital.

That same night I was living in my university halls and was having a strange dream. I dreamed that my grandmother knocked on my door and then came into the room. She told me that she was leaving but would see me again one day soon. She was wearing her best navy blue coat and carrying her best handbag. She said that she couldn't tell me where she was going but she needed to say goodbye to me.

She hugged me and then I must have woken up because the phone was ringing. It was my mum. As soon as I heard her say that she was calling about grandma I knew why. I said to mum, 'She's died hasn't she?' Mum said that she had and I told her about my strange dream. I don't know now if it was a dream or not. Perhaps she really did drop by to say her farewells and I only think that I dreamed it.

Sadie, 27

About four years ago a very dear friend of my husband and I died tragically in a car accident. At the time I was six months pregnant and we decided to call the baby Gabriella after our friend.

Gabriella (Gabby) was a really happy and outgoing child but she contracted septicaemia from having acute meningitis and died aged only seven months old. I was grief stricken as was my husband after she died. We had to arrange her funeral and inform all the family members that she had passed away.

On the morning of Gabby's funeral my husband was putting a CD into the player in the kitchen, he always said that music helps him with grief, but instead of playing the CD the machine went into radio mode and began playing a song that we had sung to Gabby that always made her laugh, *Nellie the Elephant*.

We were amazed because it's very unusual to hear a song like that on normal radio. It turned out it was an advert but we took it as a sign that Gabby was trying to contact us and tell us that she is still laughing. Both my husband and I believe very strongly in the afterlife. Since the day of her funeral we often hear her laughter coming from her old bedroom across the hall. We know that she hasn't left us for good.

Danny, 17

My mum works the night shift at a local factory and until recently a neighbour used to come and sit with me while she worked. I'm now nearly fourteen so I persuaded her that it's now OK to leave me at home on my own when she goes out to work. My dad left us when I was seven so it's just me and mum now.

One night she left for work and I was at home on my

own, I decided to go to bed early. There was nothing on TV that I wanted to watch and I had finished my homework. That night I woke up in my room convinced that I had heard a noise. I could see a tall figure standing over me and smiling sadly. All I could hear was a quiet 'Goodbye', and then the figure vanished.

The next morning I was having breakfast with mum when the phone rang. I heard my mum talking quietly then putting the receiver down. When she came back into the kitchen she was visibly upset. She told me that her brother, my Uncle Jamie, had been killed in Iraq a few hours earlier. I had always been close to Uncle Jamie who used to tell me tales of being a soldier and I knew instantly that it had been him in my bedroom the night before. He had come to say goodbye before he went into the spirit world.

Joanna, 39

My Aunt Susan died on Mother's Day 2007. I was very upset because I had always been close to her and she was always round our house or we would be round her house and there was always fun and laughter around us. Exactly twelve months to the day after her death I had a very weird dream. I was walking around the outside of Aunt Susan's house admiring the garden.

My aunt had always been a very keen gardener and her garden was beautiful, full of flowers and shrubs. I suddenly felt very calm and happy and when I looked to my right I saw Aunt Susan standing next to me smiling. She looked ageless and radiant. She put an arm around my shoulders and hugged me. I could smell her perfume and I felt the most peaceful I'd ever felt. She felt so warm and solid.

Then she pointed to her garden and told me that this is where she is. She told me to contact her children, my cousins, because they would be missing her on Mother's Day and that I should tell them that she loved them. I woke up in the morning feeling very rested. That day I spoke to my mum who had had a similar dream to me and we agreed that it was Susan telling us that she hadn't forgotten us.

Rosa, 42

Since my mum passed away last autumn she has communicated with me many times.

She knew that I was very interested in the spiritual world and I feel almost as if she is showing me around. The night she died I sat on my bed crying and suddenly felt her sit down beside me and put her arm around me. The air smelled of her and I just knew she was with me to comfort me.

When it snowed last winter I put salt on my driveway and cleared the path and the flower beds so they wouldn't freeze. It was cold and I remember telling mum that I had missed her over Christmas and asked her to give me a sign that she was still there.

The very next morning I looked out of the window and the flowerbeds were full of snowdrops. There hadn't even been any shoots the day before. Mum used to love it when the snowdrops came out at the end of winter. She always looked forward to the spring so much.

It's the little things like that that make me understand that she is still around me in some way.

Kurt, 19

My Aunt Jenni was always round our house with my cousin Matt. She was my mother's sister and there was only eighteen months between them in age so they were very close. She had a heart problem and collapsed one day and had to be taken to hospital.

The same day I was sitting in my bedroom when I heard a noise downstairs. I went out onto the landing and saw my Aunt Jenni had just come through the door. I called out 'hi,' and asked her when she left hospital but she didn't answer me and just walked on into the kitchen.

I went downstairs but when I looked into the kitchen there was no one there. About fifteen minutes later my mother phoned to tell me that my aunt had died in the hospital. What I saw must have been her spirit come to say goodbye to me.

Julia, 19

My maternal grandmother died when I was eight years old so I don't remember her very well but she was kind and gentle and loved tending her garden. After her death the whole family used to tell stories about her. I also remember that we used to visit her every week. Whatever day of the week she was all ready for us with the kettle boiling and a fresh cake. After she died we used to visit my grandfather twice a week because he was so lonely without her. I inherited her ring and I wear it all the time and I believe that she is with me because of that.

When we used to visit granddad I often used to see a lady in the garden fussing with the flowers. One day I wandered outside and the lady turned to me and smiled. It was my grandmother! She smiled at me and said 'There's a lot to do!' I saw her more often in her garden after that. The day before my granddad died she said to me, 'Not long now.'

After I heard that my granddad had died I suddenly understood, she meant that she would soon be with granddad again, or that he would be with her. After granddad died, I never saw her again.

Michaela, 42

My son, Jesse, was killed in a motoring accident in 2007 and I miss him still. Whenever I feel upset I get the sensation of someone smoothing my hair. I still keep his college scarf in his old bedroom and sometimes when I go in there it's lying on the bed instead of on the hook where I put it. Nobody goes into that room except me.

He was very keen on music and had loads of CDs. So when the radio comes on by itself I'm not surprised. It often happens in the kitchen in the morning. When Jesse would come downstairs in the morning the first thing he'd do would be to switch the radio on. For some time after his death I couldn't put the radio on in the morning because I was so full of grief.

I also find that I can smell him suddenly, out of the blue. The other day I was walking to the shops when I felt a warm breeze on my face and I knew that it was him, it was his unique smell – washing powder, soap and hair gel. The warm breeze was arresting because it was February outside and quite cold.

The coffee machine comes on when I'm in the house alone. Jesse seemed to drink about fifty cups of coffee a day. I used to wonder how he managed to sleep. About a year after he died I went with a friend to see a clairvoyant. She gave me a message from Jesse.

She said to me, 'Your son wants me to tell you that he is happy and still with you'. I think that you just have to believe and open yourself to communication from the spirit world.

Everyone I've ever talked with on the subject has some experience to tell me, even if they don't fully believe it. There are just too many coincidences for these things to be happening randomly.

Michelle, 30

When my grandmother Deirdre (known as Deedee), died I was really sad because I had been very close to her. She suffered from Alzheimer's, and died in 2006 after a period of decline. I used to love visiting her apartment. She had a particular smell that I often recall when I think about her, like roses and cinnamon.

My son was born in 2008 and I was overjoyed to become a mother. The only thing that saddened me was that my little boy would never know his great-grandma. When my son was twelve months old I was cleaning the living room having put him down for a nap in his bedroom when the smell of my grandmother overwhelmed me. I could smell the roses and cinnamon smell all around me. I looked around me but I couldn't see anything out of place.

About an hour later I went to wake up my little boy only to find him standing up in his cot giggling. He was pointing at the ceiling saying, 'Deedee, Deedee, Deedee', over and over again. I said to him who is Deedee? And he pointed to the ceiling again, clapped his hands and chuckled. He was in a very jolly mood for the rest of the day and when I put him to bed he was still giggling and calling out, 'Deedee!' I couldn't help but smile myself.

As I shut his bedroom door I once again felt surrounded by roses and cinnamon smells and I clearly heard my grandmother's voice inside my head saying, 'I'm so glad you've found happiness'.

I really felt that it was her letting me know that everything would be OK. My son still calls to 'Deedee,' and I take great comfort in the fact that my grandmother did meet my little boy in the end.

Theresa, 17

My dad is keen on DIY and needed to get his electric saw sharpened so that he could put up some shelves in my bedroom. The man he goes to for this type of job is my friend Charlotte's granddad who mends tools at his house. I sometimes go with him so I can hang out with Charlotte because she lives just across the street but on this particular occasion I didn't because she was on vacation with her parents.

According to my dad, he went round to Charlotte's granddad's house but when he knocked on the door there was no answer. He waited a while and then walked around the property to see if there was anyone else in.

Sensing a movement behind him he turned to see an elderly man waving at him. The man then disappeared through the back gate. He was a fair distance away but my dad thought that this man looked very much like Charlotte's granddad. However, when he shouted to him there was no response. The man seemed to have disappeared.

The next day, Charlotte came back from her vacation. I was surprised because she was supposed to be away all week. She told me that the reason that she'd come back early was because a neighbour had phoned to tell them that her grandfather had collapsed, and was in hospital.

Unfortunately he died before they got there. The time of death was the exact time that my dad had seen the old man wave to him. Although he is very sceptical of these things he does wonder if the man he saw was the spirit of Charlotte's grandfather saying goodbye.

Carrie, 32

I'm now thirty-two and I got married two years ago. I've always regretted the fact that my granddad never met my husband, Ralph, and wasn't able to come to the wedding.

On the day itself I was very nervous as I got ready but suddenly I felt something warm on my arm. I looked but there was nothing to see. The pressure on my arm wasn't scary; it was more comforting if anything. It was then that I smelled the unmistakable smell of his hair oil.

I knew then that it was my granddad wishing me well on my big day. I could smell the familiar scent right the way up to the altar. I could swear that I also felt my granddad next to me as Ralph and I exchanged vows.

When I asked Ralph later if he had noticed anything he was just bewildered, but I know that I did. My granddad came to my wedding after all and I know that his message was that he was happy with me and wished both me and my husband well.

Billy, 34

My grandfather passed away about two years ago and I have always missed him since. He used to be very good at playing the piano and was always playing songs from musicals like *Cats* or *Phantom of the Opera*. Just before Christmas this year I was feeling very sad when suddenly an advertisement came on TV playing the theme tune from *Phantom of the Opera*. I just knew that it was my grandfather communicating with me by playing something I would remember him playing.

I now know that whenever I hear any song from a musical that it is my grandfather saying 'Hello,' to me.

Laura, 18

My brother died of a drug overdose when he was twenty-five. He had got in with a bad group of friends and began abusing alcohol before moving on to harder drugs, eventually taking heroin by the time he was twenty-one. He did try a treatment programme about four months before he died but the methadone left him feeling depressed and in desperation he took some heroin at his girlfriend's house.

His girlfriend wasn't there when his body was found and the autopsy showed that he had died from mixing a large dose of methadone with a similarly large dose of

Brandon, 45

Before we married, my wife came to spend Christmas with me, bringing her two children, aged five and eight, from her previous marriage with her. Late one night we were talking about getting married; we were both a little reluctant because we had both come out of unhappy marriages.

That night I dreamt of a beautiful African woman in a red dress who turned to me and nodded and smiled. The dream was so vivid that I told my girlfriend (now my wife), about it the next day.

As I described the woman she stared at me in disbelief. She then told me that I had seen her mother who had passed away several years earlier. Her mother had been buried in her favourite red dress. We took this as a sign from her mother that we should go ahead and get married. We celebrated our wedding day the following June.

Ingrid, 45

My daughter Elise was killed in a skiing accident when she was only eighteen. Since she died I have had a lot of strange dreams that took place in a remote village in the mountains, where I grew up. Down the road I see a procession of young girls in long white dresses walking in twos and holding hands.

As they pass me one of them smiles at me and I realise that it is Elise but before I can talk to her she walks past. I run after her until she eventually turns and we have a big hug. I ask her how she is and she tells me that she is very happy and that she has made many friends. She also tells me that I can't be with her yet.

When I woke up from these dreams I would feel much better. Still grieving but with a little thought at the back of my mind that Elise was OK and I had to get on with my life until I could join her. I think that in order to accept that someone has died we need to understand that they are not lost forever, that we will see them again. I've had other dreams where Elise is telling me not to worry because she will always come back to me.

She loved the spring primroses and I always pick her a bunch for her grave. The last time I put flowers on her grave I heard her voice. She said, 'You know it's always spring'. I puzzled over that for a while but then thought that she was telling me about where she was now. Spring was her favourite time of year and she was letting me know that she lived somewhere now where it was always spring.

Pritti, 50

Our daughter, Surinder, died of ovarian cancer when she was just thirty-three years old. She left two children, an eight-year-old boy and a six-year-old girl behind. I always had a special relationship with Surinder. Perhaps deep down I somehow knew that she wouldn't be around me for long.

One time when she was a little girl we went to our local mother and baby club so that she could play with other children, this was something we did when the weather was too bad to be outside for a long time.

We drove a funny old car, a Morris I think it was, and on that day, when we got home she began shouting at me to park on the other side of the street. I was so startled that I did what she asked, just before the strong winds broke off a huge branch from the tree that fell down at the exact spot where I usually parked the car.

It was just before New Year in 1998 that Surinder was diagnosed with ovarian cancer. We were all so shocked by the news. She had told us that she was feeling very tired but as the mother of two young children we thought it was just part of the territory. Over the next twelve months, she had two operations, radiotherapy and chemotherapy but nothing worked. The cancer spread very fast and the doctors told us that it was a very aggressive form of tumour.

The weeks after her death are a blur; I do remember we looked after our grandchildren every day while their dad was at work. We had them overnight during weekdays to help him out as he worked long shifts. I eventually realised that Molly, the youngest child was chattering away in her sleep, to 'mummy'.

The next morning she would tell me that mummy had

been to visit her to make sure that she was happy with granny. I asked her how often she saw her mummy and she told me that it was every night after I turned the light out. She seemed so assured about this that I felt a little strange. And of course I remembered Surinder's psychic powers as a child.

One night I crept up to her bedroom door when heard her chattering, and saw her sitting on the end of her bed waving her toy elephant into the darkness and then giggling. When I went into the room and looked at her face, her eyes looked like the eyes of a sleepwalker.

She was playing in her sleep with someone I couldn't see. The next morning I asked if she had slept well and she told me that she had been playing with Elmer (the elephant), and mummy. I think Surinder has passed her psychic gift to her daughter and I'm happy that Molly hasn't lost her mother completely.

Kate, 20

When I was a little girl, my Auntie Vivienne lived in our house with us. She died when I was three or four years old and I don't really remember her, but I do know that we were very close. I remember looking at her dead body on the bed and seeing what looked like white fog floating upwards from her body.

Then I dreamed that my aunt woke me up from my bed and took me outside to the little garden at the back of our house. My Auntie Vivienne picked a peach coloured rose and showed it to me. She told me that heaven was like the flowers in the garden, beautiful and carefree. She said that she was happy in heaven and that we shouldn't worry about her.

When I woke up I told my mum about the dream and took her outside to show her the flower. There was just one peach coloured rose lying on the grass. It was the one my auntie had picked in my dream the night before.

Deborah, 39

My sister, Anna, died in 2004 at the age of forty-six, after fighting cancer for nearly two years. She was the oldest of three sisters and had always been so strong and outgoing. She was the kind of person that everyone loved. She was really good fun to be around with a big heart and kind words.

In the weeks before she died, Anna was bedridden, too weak to walk and in a lot of pain. The cancer had got into her lungs and she was finding it hard to breathe. A couple of days before she died I was passing her room and I heard her saying, 'Mum, Hello Mum.' Our mother had died from cancer herself at forty years old. I looked into the room and saw Anna staring at the wall with unfocused eyes calling out for mum.

The next day I asked her how she felt and she told me that mum had been to see her and that she was with God.

Anna died that night. I believe that our mother came back to tell Anna that she would be joining her too. I find great comfort in this. I know now that one day I will be with both of them again in heaven.

David, 45

My best friend, Kenny, shot himself in 1998. He was studying for his final law exams at the time. I was at work when my wife telephoned me to tell me what had happened. We were both very upset because we loved him very much. Apparently he had found out that his wife was having an affair and wanted to leave him. He had drunk a bottle of whisky and then shot himself in the garage.

His wife was devastated and insisted that the affair was a mistake and that she'd loved him and never wanted to leave him. Three years later, she had still not remarried and as I was sleeping I had a dream that Kenny came to my bedside and told me to pass on a message to his wife.

He said that he had been watching her and knew how sorry she was for her actions and wanted me to tell her that he wanted her to stop punishing herself. He said I should tell her that it was fine for her to remarry and be happy. I told her and the following summer she remarried.

They now have a little boy who she's named Kenny after her first love.

Deanna, 24

My father was diagnosed with terminal cancer about three years ago. After his diagnosis we talked about life after death and I said that if there was a way to come back and contact us from the other side that he should try to do so and let me know that he was OK.

He died a year after his diagnosis and, although I knew it was coming, his actual passing left me very upset. I went to stay with my older sister for a while. One night when I was watching a late night movie on TV I felt a rush of cold air and a definite smell of my father. A kind of tobacco mixed with cologne sort of smell.

I looked behind me and my father was sitting in the armchair. He looked so much healthier than he had at the end of his life and he smiled at me and said, 'See, I told you I'd do it'. Just as suddenly as he appeared he disappeared again and the temperature in the room went back to normal.

Debbie, 17

My best friend Dean passed away in a car crash in 2009. It was strange because the weekend before he died I had met him and he was just glowing. There was something different about him that made your attention linger on him. That was on the Friday as school closed for the weekend.

On the following Sunday evening we got the call that he had been killed. He had been driving home from his cousin's house with his mum and dad when a large truck swerved into their lane and crushed the car. His mom had also been killed and his dad was seriously injured in hospital.

I couldn't stop thinking about how special he had looked. Over the next few nights I found it hard to sleep, I was really upset about my friend's death. Then one night I woke up to find him sitting on my bed. He told me that it was great to see me again and we talked about school and our friends.

As we were having this conversation, I suddenly remembered that he had passed on and wondered why he was talking to me in my room. I asked him and he told me that he knew he had died but that he wanted to say goodbye to me one last time. He pushed a four leafed clover into my hand and told me it was for luck.

When I awoke the next morning I wasn't sure whether or not I had dreamed the nights events. Then I looked down to where I'd put my trainers under the dresser the night before and I saw next to them a small crushed up piece of clover.

Darren, 32

My granddad died from throat cancer four years ago and just after he died I went to stay with my grandma because she was very upset by my grandfather's death. She hadn't lived alone for forty years. My granddad had died at home with his family around him and though his passing was sad we were all grateful that at least he hadn't died alone.

One night I woke up sensing that something was going on. It wasn't that I could hear anything. It was more that I felt like there was someone else in the house besides me and grandma. I got up and went downstairs to have a look around but it was all still and quiet. I checked the doors and windows and they were all locked so I went back upstairs.

I peeped into my grandma's room and she was in bed sleeping but then I noticed that there was another figure in the bed. My granddad was lying in bed next to her. I couldn't believe what I was seeing but it was definitely him. I was too scared to wake my grandma in case it upset her so I went back to the bedroom where I was staying. I must have dozed off for a while because the next thing I knew my granddad was standing by my bed.

He leaned down and said to me, 'Thank you for staying with May (my grandma's name), I'm very proud of you. Tell your gran that I love her very much and I will always be next to her until she joins me in the afterlife. I will always be watching over you all'.

When I woke up the next morning I told my grandma everything that had happened during the night. My grandma said it was probably just a vivid dream but when I told her the message from my granddad her eyes filled with tears. She told me that sometimes she did feel as if my granddad was with her at night.

Greta, 20

I lost my dad in a road accident about two years ago and because it was all so sudden I found it really hard to cope. In the weeks after his death all I wanted to do was lie in bed ignoring everyone and everything. My mum and sister were trying to get me to eat but I didn't want to. I didn't even wash my hair. The whole family was grieving badly but I seemed to have taken it worse than anyone else.

About four weeks after dad died I was lying in bed when I distinctly heard a voice whispering in my ear. 'It's time for you to let go.' I looked around my room but there was no one there. I even went into my sister's room to check that she wasn't playing a joke with me.

When I went back into my room and lay down again I heard the voice again. It was a woman's voice, very soft and kind. She said, 'Let him go'. I knew then that she was talking about my dad, and there was life after death, I would see him again one day. I had to get on with my life and leave him to go into heaven.

I slept better that night than I had in weeks and the next morning I felt a little better. I wasn't over it by any standards, but able to cope with simple tasks which I hadn't been able to do before. And I realised that I was being self-indulgent, because I was allowing myself to collapse while my mother and sister were having to deal with all the practical problems. From that day I started trying to help out more and I could see that they saw that as a big improvement.

I have gradually been getting better in the last two years and although I still miss him I can enjoy my life now and again. When you lose someone it is a strange thing because you reach a point where you think you are over it. But then one little thing sends you back to square one. you find yourself listening to an old song on the radio and dissolving in tears. But it does get easier over time, and the difficult times get further apart.

Tim, 26

When I still lived at home with my parents we were in an apartment block on the second floor. At ground level there was an elderly lady who was confined to a wheel-chair. My friends and I used to call her 'the witch' because she was quite bad-tempered and didn't seem to want to be friends with any of the neighbours. She was often sitting out in the communal gardens outside the front of our block and although she would occasionally nod a 'hello' that was all you got generally.

I remember one day my family was talking around the dinner table. We talked about how we hadn't seen her for a while and wondered if she had moved away. That night

I had a dream about the old lady. She was no longer in a wheel chair and she came into my bedroom to tell me that she was sorry for being so bad-tempered. She told me that she had died and that she was much happier now because she could walk.

The next weekend we saw some people clearing out her apartment and my dad went over to chat with them. They told him that the old lady had died two weeks earlier in hospital.

Nadia, 54

My mother died in 1998 after having suffered a series of strokes. I was with her at the hospital on her last day but she died in the early hours of the morning and I wasn't with her then. I cried for a long time after her passing, we had been very close and I really missed her.

About a month later I awoke to find her sitting by my bed. She told me that heaven is a wonderful place and she is very happy there. She said that she had come back to comfort me because she couldn't bear to see me being so unhappy. I don't even know if I dreamed it or not but it was unlike any dream I'd ever had.

My mother looked so beautiful and healthy and was wearing a long red dress. I could smell her and feel her presence in a very solid way. When I woke up the next morning I felt comforted because I felt as if she had come to me because she still cared about me so much.

Molly, 45

When I was a little girl, about nine or so, I used to go to stay with my grandmother at weekends when my mum and dad went out for dinner with friends. She was always lovely to me and we'd bake cakes and have fun looking through old photographs and boxes of her old costume jewellery from the 1930s and 1940s.

I slept in the room that had been my mother's when she was a little girl and even after I'd been sent to bed I would sometimes sneakily get up to look through my mum's bookcase. On this particular night I remember reading on the rug with the lamp on when I heard my grandmother calling my name.

She was saying, 'Molly, Molly come here'. I went into her bedroom and saw her asleep. Then I heard her voice again. She said 'It's not me there; I'm gone but always remember me. I love you very much. Now, go and get granddad and tell him'. I was confused but went to my granddad's room and woke him up to tell him that he had to go to grandma.

It turned out that my grandma had died. She wasn't asleep, she was gone. Although I was so sad that I had lost her I believe that she spoke to me that night to let me know how much she loved me. I feel her with me still and I feel special because she came to me at her time of death to say goodbye.

Lara, 24

My fiancé was killed in a car crash about six months ago and I was devastated. He had given me a bracelet the previous year when we were on holiday and I wore it day and night.

One morning last week I woke up and when I went to touch the bracelet on my wrist as I do every morning it wasn't there. I immediately searched the bed sheets but couldn't find it.

I had a shower praying that it would turn up. When I went back into my bedroom to get dressed the bracelet was lying on top of my bedcover. At the same time I felt as if someone was giving me a gentle hug. I think my fiancé came back to me for a few moments that day.

Luella, 24

My family are from Mexico and when my grandmother who still lives there was ill, my mum went over there to look after her until she was well enough to look after herself. Not long after my mum arrived there my grandmother was diagnosed with bowel cancer and the doctors weren't optimistic about her chances of recovery.

My mum extended her stay because she wanted to be with her mother to the very end. About five weeks after my mum told me the bad news about my grandmother I had a dream about her. In the dream my grandmother was with my grandfather who had passed away the year before.

Granddad said to me that he had gone to collect grandma because he was lonely without her. My grandmother just smiled at me and said 'It's time to go now. Bye, bye.'

I was woken the next morning at about 7am because the phone was ringing. Before I answered it I already knew what the news was going to be. It was my mum on the phone and I said, 'She's died hasn't she?' My mum confirmed that my grandmother had died during the night. I told her about my dream and mum said that she had been sitting by my grandmother's bed and my grandma said my granddad's name in her sleep just before she died.

Psychic Phenomena, Clairvoyance and Clairaudience

Seeing and hearing from the dead

For some, the ability to communicate with the dead is not limited to the spirits of people they met and knew in this world. There are those for whom talking to the dead has become a profession or an engrossing hobby and gift.

This section includes accounts from people who can see and/or hear the dead and demonstrates the variety of means by which this communication is possible. These people may have a connection with relatives who died long before they were born. Some can communicate through a variety of electronic devices. While in other cases, simply by meditating, they can have an audience with spirits in the afterlife.

Janine, 23

From a very early age I have been seeing ghosts. When I was a child they would appear at night and stand around my bed. One frequent visitor was an elderly lady with her hair in a bun. Another was a small boy who was always crying. At first it was terrifying and eventually I told my mum. She asked me to describe the old lady and when I did she turned quite pale and went upstairs to her bedroom.

When she returned she showed me a photograph and it was the exact same woman! It was my grandmother who I didn't remember because she died when I was just a baby. My mum explained that she had had cancer and knew that she was dying and it upset her to think that she'd never see me grow up.

She was returning to watch over me as I slept. She still visits me and I don't find it frightening any more, I give her a smile now and then go to sleep. I think she's telling me that she's watching over me and taking care of me.

Clare, 31

My eight-year-old son has told me that he often sees two men, he calls them Wizzy and Ziggy. He says that Wizzy is very jolly and turns up whenever my son is playing and having fun. The other man Ziggy appears only when my son is upset. Wizzy claps and cheers if my son is winning a game or just messing around as boys do and Ziggy smiles gently at him when he is unhappy.

He enjoys seeing both men but I have no idea who they are. Last week we went to our local woods for a picnic and my son said to me that Wizzy was with us and that meant that we were going to have fun.

When we got to our usual picnic spot I found my sister there also picnicking with her six-year-old son. We all had a lovely afternoon as my sister and I chatted while our boys climbed trees. I'm not sure if Wizzy and Ziggy are ghosts or spirits but they do seem to make my son very happy.

Conrad, 34

Some years ago, after losing my beloved grandfather I went to see a clairvoyant who managed to contact him. The clairvoyant said that my grandfather was holding an old fashioned chocolate box, and hinted that it was important that I find it.

She also told me that the box was in my mother's house but had been forgotten about as we sorted and cleared out my grandfather's house. I went to see my mother and told her the message we had got from the clairvoyant and she began to search for the chocolate box.

When she found it we were astonished at what was inside. There were details of several bank accounts and a will leaving the money to be shared between me and my mother. My mum was a single mum and had worked hard during my childhood to provide for me. It was such a lovely gift to receive from beyond the grave and although I was initially suspicious, I am really glad that I saw that clairvoyant.

Martha, 48

I went to see a medium just for fun with a friend. I don't usually believe in these things and was convinced it would just be a load of hoky poky. Earlier in my life I had loved painting landscapes but had stopped when I became a mother as looking after the kids took up most of my time.

During my session with the medium, she described a woman who I knew instantly was my great-aunt Sarah who had died three years earlier. The clairvoyant told me that my great-aunt was holding a paintbrush in her hands and telling me to use it. I was amazed, my aunt Sarah had always been very supportive of my painting and it was as if she was telling me to get back to it.

My children are now aged 16 and 18 and are less demanding of my time so I thought it was perhaps a good time to revive my old hobby. I have since had a gallery opening and have sold four paintings, bringing in much needed new income!

Graham, 31

For the last ten years I have been able to contact the spirits of dead people. In every single incident I can hear music coming from an electrical device such as a computer or radio, even when it is switched off. After that I start to see spirits in my mind and they start to talk, just as if they were having a normal conversation with me.

As the years go by my gift gets stronger. I am able to ask the spirits questions which I'm told is quite rare as most psychic people only receive messages from the dead.

Some spirits are calm and easy to talk to and others can be quite aggressive. In general I find that evil spirits give up trying to contact me if a good spirit arrives for a conversation. I have even had a group of spirits looking amazed and discussing who I am.

Amy, 29

Over the last few years strange things have been happening in our house and my seven-year-old daughter Lucy says her granddad and his mother, (her great grand-mother), who are both dead, are living under her bed and come out to play with her at night.

I asked her why and she told me that her granddad said he is here because he's dead and can now take care of her properly. I have to say, I'm a bit spooked by this.

It seems that as Lucy gets older the visits become less and less frequent and will hopefully peter out as she grows up. The thing is, she is able to describe them perfectly even though they died before she was born.

Anna, 35

About three years ago, when I lived in a small town, I had some strange experiences with the apartment that I then lived in. It was on the third floor and I had some very good neighbours who all looked out for each other.

One night at around nine o'clock, I was out with some friends after work when a neighbour, Julie (a kind single woman who lived above me on the fourth floor with her two kids) called my cellphone to tell me that she was taking the garbage out and claimed to have looked up and saw a strange woman walking past the window in my apartment.

She told me that the woman came back to the window and then looked out at her. She looked up, presumed I must have a guest staying with me, and went back inside her own apartment. However, at around eight or so, she claimed she heard some pounding on the ceiling at her. It was so loud that it sounded as if it were being done with a hammer. She panicked, thinking that there must be something wrong, and phoned my apartment from her own phone. When nobody answered the phone she feared the worst and immediately ran upstairs to try the apartment door. When she couldn't get an answer she called my cell and so I found myself rushing home to find out what was going on.

When I reached my apartment I was trembling as I put the key in the lock, not knowing what I would find inside. When I switched on the light in the hallway, there was no one around and nothing had been moved. I checked all the rooms and the exit onto the fire escape but it seemed clear to me that nobody had been in my apartment while I was out. This seemed very strange, but eventually Julie and I decided to accept that we didn't know what she had seen or heard but nothing appeared to have happened in my apartment, so for now all was well. However, this wasn't the end of it.

On the third floor, opposite me, there's a young guy, Jake, and his girlfriend Sarah who's pregnant. His girlfriend claimed that she opened her door and saw a woman at the end of our hall wearing a grey plaid skirt, staring out of the window. She had never seen the woman before but said hello to her. The woman never answered her or turned round from the window.

A couple of weeks later, Julie said that she was passing by my door and knew that I had left for work, because my car was gone. She had just returned home from her job at the deli. She told me that she could hear a woman crying inside my apartment. She began to speculate that my apartment was haunted. To be honest, I'd begun to worry about it by then. Until then I'd never had anything unusual happen inside my apartment but one night not long after that I swear someone bumped the end of my bed when I was half asleep. Then after a few minutes the bed pressed down beside me as if someone was sitting on it

Eventually, I decided to try to find out what was going on. I went to the local library to look up what exactly happened inside our building. In 1948, a woman had been stabbed to death by a stranger who had broken in the apartment that was now mine, through the fire escape door. The murderer had escaped and never been caught.

All over town, people started getting extra security locks on their doors, fearful that something like this would happen again. I couldn't find a picture of the woman who had died but she seemed to be the same age as the woman who my neighbours had seen in my apartment.

I was puzzled however, as to why she had decided to make herself visible to people now. No one had ever reported seeing her before. My neighbours suggested that she might be warning me to make sure I was safe.

The following weekend the local paper ran a story about a rapist who had attacked two women separately in their apartments late at night. I decided to check my doors and windows; the weird thing is that when I came to examine the fire door, the lock simply broke off in my hand. It wasn't secure at all. I had never used it since I'd moved to the apartment so had never realised that it wasn't secure. I immediately called a locksmith who mended it. No one ever saw the murdered woman again. I do believe now that she was telling me to check that I was safe. It's comforting in a way to know that.

Sophia, 54

In 2003, my husband Ken died from cancer. He had been in the hospital a long time and when he died, at four in the morning, I was by his bedside. The nurses had called me the previous evening to tell me that he was extremely poorly and may not survive the night. I went there immediately and kept vigil by his bedside.

After making arrangements with the nurses as to the funeral home arrangements I went home. It was about 6.30 in the morning by then. Feeling too upset to sleep I made coffee and sat at the kitchen table, making lists of all the people I would need to contact that day.

At 7.35, the phone rang and a voice that sounded really like Ken's asked me 'Sophia, why are you still at home? I am waiting for you.' The phone then went dead. This really disturbed me because before he died, I always went to visit him every morning before work at 7.30am. Because he had died at 4am, I wasn't with him at 7.30 that morning.

I was very curious about what had actually happened and a few months later I went to see a medium. He told me that there is sometimes a gap between a person dying and their reaching the other side. Apparently this happens most often when someone dies in their sleep. He believed that my husband's spirit was still in the hospital room confused as to why I wasn't visiting him.

The medium then told me that Ken was now happy and still with me every day loving me very much.

Bryan, 29

I film my father when he visits me. You might think that's nothing unusual but if I tell you that he died in 1996 then you'll begin to see that this is a surprising tale. When he died I was in my teens and at that stage where you seem to always be at war with your parents. He was killed suddenly in a car accident. Over the next few years I was saddened that I hadn't made up with him properly before he died. I think he also felt that he had unfinished business with me because he certainly makes his presence felt from time to time.

After he died, my mum gave me his video camera and when I was 21 and got my own apartment, I took it with me. I left it on the dresser in my sitting room. One night as I was watching TV the camera suddenly began to whir and hum: the camera had turned itself on.

The thought that my dad might have done it did cross my mind but I dismissed it as being too far-fetched. However, later the same evening two smoke detectors began beeping at the same time even though there was no smoke and the lamps began to flicker slightly as if the power to them was being interfered with.

I went to bed sure that it must just be a localised electricity problem but the biggest shock was what happened the next morning.

As I was getting ready for work, the building supervisor knocked on my door and asked who my visitor was who had been ringing to get into my apartment at 2am? I told him that I'd been asleep by then and that nobody had rung the bell but he told me that they had and that it had been caught on the security tapes over the front entrance.

When I went downstairs and saw the tapes I was stunned. The pictures were grainy and none too clear but I felt sure that the figure standing there was my father. I mumbled something non-committal to the supervisor and went back upstairs where I put a tape into the video camera and switched it on.

Nothing happened that day or evening or the next but on the evening of the third day I had a breakthrough. I was watching TV again when the smoke alarms went off again. There was no smoke but as I went into the kitchen to check, the microwave started up. I switched it off and went back to the living room and sat down again. Apart from a strange static feeling in the air I could see nothing. I was watching my favourite team and so just settled down to watch.

When the match was over the room seemed much lighter and on a whim I rewound the tape in the video recorder to see if anything had happened. What I saw took my breath away. There were strange blurry areas on the film of the room and they were moving. Eventually the blur seemed to sit beside me on the sofa. Although I couldn't see for sure I believe that the blur was my dad's spirit come to sit and watch the match with me since we couldn't do it in real life any more.

There have been many times since when he's visited me and on those days the smoke alarms and other electrical gadgets in the apartment always go a bit funny. Always when I check the tape the blur is there on the film while there's nothing on the days when I don't feel his presence. Some of my friends think I'm nuts but I feel comforted in a way. I feel as if I've made up with my dad after his death. It feels so nice to have got a second chance like that. I'd say I was blessed.

Tammy, 38

I have a co-worker, Mary, who claims that she's psychic. Not long ago she told me that when she came into work one morning she could see an elderly lady standing behind me and she had known instantly that it was my grandmother. I was shocked because my grandmother had died six months earlier. It had to be her though because Mary's description of her was spot on. She told me that my grandmother was showing her a white painted house. I was actually in the process of finding a new house and had narrowed it down to two houses I had viewed and one of them was painted white.

My grandmother lived in the state of Indiana in a white house and I had spent many summers there with her. The house had jasmine growing up the walls and it smelled wonderful. Mary told me that my grandmother wanted me to live in the white house to remember her and that she was still with me, helping me. I am now in the process of buying the white house and I'm going to plant some jasmine outside so that whenever I smell it I'll think of my grandmother.

Raff, 36

I had a strange encounter while driving on the highway with my daughter Chloe. As we drove along Chloe suddenly let out a scream and said 'we need to call an ambulance.' I asked her why but she just kept saying that the ambulance had to hurry or the man would die.

About five minutes later I heard sirens and an ambulance sped past us. As we rounded the bend I could see that there had been a car accident. Later that evening the local news informed us that there had been a collision on the highway and one man had died. Chloe said that she heard the dead man telling her to call an ambulance. It must have been just after the crash but I was still a bit bewildered as to whether or not my daughter could have received messages from a dead man.

Kate, 15

I am a high school student at the moment and I have had some strange experiences recently. The other day I got off the bus to see someone who looked just like me going into the school building ahead of me. I hadn't seen her before and I remember wondering who she was.

Later that day as I was walking down the corridor a girl came up to me and told me to stop flirting with her boyfriend. I was puzzled by this because I didn't know the girl or her boyfriend.

At lunch when I sat in the cafeteria a boy threw a glass of water at me and said it was revenge for me doing the same to one of his paintings in art class. I don't study art!

It was a terrible day and I was really glad to get home. However, when I told my mother about the weird things that had been going on, she went very quiet. She told me that I had had a twin sister who had only lived for a couple of weeks after birth.

She had never told me in case it upset me but that particular day was the anniversary of the death of my twin sister and my mother had been thinking about her all day. I think she wanted to come to school with me.

I now talk to her a lot and think that she is with me. I do tell her that she must only do nice things and not get me into trouble again.

Beattie, 45

Since I was a little girl I have had premonitions and been able to talk with people who have passed away. In 1992 I gave birth to a little boy called Bobby and I knew from the moment I held him in my arms that he wouldn't be with me very long. I told the doctors at the hospital but they wouldn't believe me.

A few weeks after I brought Bobby home I could tell something was wrong. He was crying all the time and the back of his head looked kind of strange. I took him back to the hospital where they did a CT scan on his brain. The scan showed that he had a tumour. The doctors told me it was inoperable.

Bobby passed away two weeks later. I was devastated and deeply in grief for many months. A friend suggested that I go to see a medium so that I could try to connect with my little boy. She recommended one that a friend of hers had seen and who she thought was very good and authentic. I was very nervous on my way to the mediums house. My friend came with me. The medium whose name was Jerry was very relaxed and friendly and instantly put me at ease. We sat around a table as he asked the spirit of Bobby to contact him.

After a few seconds his face changed shape slightly and he began to sway slightly. He then told me that Bobby was showing him a white blanket. I was astonished because I had always wrapped him in a white blanket. He told Jerry that he loved being cuddled in the blankets. I could feel myself beginning to feel tearful.

However, Jerry told me that Bobby was still with me and I could cuddle him whenever I wanted. Bobby also told that it was OK now for me to redecorate his bedroom. I hadn't been able to bring myself to change anything since he had died. Jerry said that Bobby promised to leave me more signs that he was still with me. I left feeling better than I had in a long time.

From that day on Bobby has sent me little signs. Things get moved around the house. My coffee mug turned up in the hall cupboard and I lost my watch and found it under the kitchen sink. It's these little things that have made me smile again. I can talk to Bobby whenever I want now and he always gives me a sign so that I know he is listening.

Stephanie, 19

I never knew my maternal grandmother because she died when my own mother was just 15 years old. One night, I was walking home after going out with friends and was about to step into the street to cross over when I felt a firm hand holding my shoulder.

When I look over my shoulder I just had a fleeting glimpse of a lilac dress with white flowers printed on it and a strong smell of perfume. Immediately afterwards, it was obvious that there was nothing there. At the same moment a car came out of nowhere travelling at tremendous speed. If I had stepped out into the street I would have been killed.

The following weekend I was browsing in a department store when I suddenly smelled the smell I had smelled as I attempted to cross the road earlier in the week. I asked a sales assistant what it was and was told that it was a perfume by Lanvin. On a whim I bought some for myself. On the Sunday I went round to my mum's house for lunch and she sniffed the air and said, 'Do you know you smell just how my mother used to smell?' And she correctly identified the perfume I was wearing.

I told her about the incident by the road and about the lilac flowery fabric. She told me that she remembered that dress as being one of her mother's favourites. When I was born she wished that her mother had been alive to see me and often thought about how much she would have enjoyed playing with me. Perhaps she has been with me all along.

Chantelle, 28

One night recently I couldn't get to sleep. At 2.30 in the morning I was tossing and turning with lots of random thoughts and whisperings in my head. I couldn't properly hear what the whisperings said but it sounded as if lots of people were talking at once.

I suddenly became aware of some sort of presence in the room. Then, the mattress sagged beside me as if someone had sat down on the bed. I couldn't see anything but still got the vague sensation of a presence in the room. I was very scared and actually called out, 'Who's there?' I did eventually fall asleep but was perturbed by the night's experiences all day.

The following day my ex-husband telephoned me to tell me that one of our closest friends, Julia, had died. I had become really good friends with Julia when my husband and I lived in London. She was like a big sister to me and since my mother lived some distance away in Newcastle, Julia often took care of me. My ex-husband told me that

She had died around 2.30am after having been attacked earlier in the evening as she was going home after a night out with friends. Apparently she had been discovered by a group of passers-by who alerted the medical services and got her taken to hospital.

When he told me this I realised that this was the night when I couldn't get to sleep. The whispered voices must have been me hearing the people who found her talking about what they should do, then the hospital staff as they tried to save her. She was thinking about me when she died.

Christine, 43

I've been visiting mediums for about twelve years now and I've had so many wonderful readings. My most memorable reading was about a year ago. We had a very special friend of the family that we all called 'aunt'. She was like a mother to my mom and when she died of cancer two years ago we were all extremely sad.

At this particular reading the medium gave me a very precise description of my aunt, both physically and in terms of her personality. It really was very accurate. The medium told me that my aunt was telling her to ask me to look at page six of the newspaper in my handbag. I got out the newspaper and turned to page six.

The headline was 'Linda is Full of Love'. I felt amazed because I hadn't ventured the name of my aunt nor had the medium said it. My aunt was called Linda.

Owen, 36

Ever since I moved into the house where I now live, I've been communicating with the dead. I bought this house in 1999 with some money left to me by my grandfather. It's an old house built in the 1890s with high ceilings and large fireplaces. I work as a freelance journalist so needed a room to use as my office where I could store my files and computer. This house had a great room in the attic, being at the top of the house it was very quiet with a lovely view over the tree tops in the garden.

The day after I moved in I set up my computer, modem (this was before mass broadband internet), and my filing cabinet. As I was setting everything up, there seemed to be a weird sensation in the air, like the way the atmosphere feels just before a huge thunderstorm. At the time I put it down to my tiredness from having moved house.

That night as I lay in bed trying to sleep I heard a strange dragging noise coming from the ceiling above me. The room above my bedroom is the attic office. I then heard a creaking sound as if someone was sitting down at my desk chair. It's always been a bit creaky. I bought it from a second hand office supply store years ago and had never replaced it.

My first thought was that there was an intruder in my house. I don't handle sensitive information in my job as a journalist so I couldn't think who would want my office files. I grabbed my old baseball bat that I had kept since high school and headed up the second flight of stairs. Through the doorway I could see the light from my screen-saver and I crept quietly to the door.

However, when I peeped round the door there was no one there. I edged quietly into the room but couldn't see any sign that anybody had been inside there. I have one of those screensavers that have scrolling words, you can write whatever you want and the message scrolls across the screen in various colours. My screensaver always said 'Get back to work!' because I'm such a procrastinator even when I have an urgent deadline. I always end up working through the night to get the job done.

This time though, when I glanced at the screen, the words, 'Hi, hi, hi' were scrolling. I thought it must be someone having a practical joke with me but couldn't think who could have done it. My assistant had dropped by at lunchtime with some documents for me but as far as I knew she hadn't been upstairs to this room.

I shut down the computer and went back to sleep. The next day I switched on the computer to start work and went downstairs to get some coffee. When I got back the screen-saver was running. It said 'friendly, friendly, friendly.' I was puzzled but had to get to work so I wrote through the morning and then went out for lunch.

When I came back to the house my garbage cab had been emptied all over the porch. Presuming that it was kids or dogs I cleaned it up, cursing under my breath. When everything was back to being neat and tidy, I went back up to my office.

Out of habit now I looked at the screen-saver. The words 'friendly, friendly, friendly', were rolling round the monitor again. This was beginning to be very weird. I finished what I was doing, filed my papers away for the day and went down to the kitchen to start supper.

When I opened the refrigerator there was an overwhelming smell of rotting food. The milk had gone sour, the cheese mouldy green and the yoghurts looked swollen and ready to burst. I shut the door and checked the connection. The refrigerator had been switched off. Outside in the garden, flowers had been uprooted and the water from the tap just dripped with a brown dirty drizzle. I couldn't help shouting, 'What is going on?'

Suddenly, I had this overwhelming urge to go up to my office room and I ran up the stairs, two at a time. This time the screensaver read, 'friend?' I was exasperated so just said out loud, 'OK, I'm your friend'.

When I said that the air seemed to lighten and the whole house seemed brighter. I went to look out of the window for a second and when I turned to the computer, the words had changed. The single word 'Happy' was scrolling left to right across the screen. Nothing bad happened over the next few weeks, but I wondered about the messages on the computer.

At one point, I was raking leaves in the yard, and my next door neighbour introduced himself to me over the fence. He had lived in his house for seventy years, since he was a little boy, and seemed very nice although I hadn't really spoken to him at length at that point. His name was Ben and he asked me how I was settling in. As we chatted I couldn't help but mention the strange messages on my computer and he nodded as if he was sure he knew what was causing them.

He explained to me that a little boy called Jimmy had died in the house when he was twelve years old. His bedroom had been the attic room that was now my office. Apparently the boy died of pneumonia in 1960 after spending a long amount of time in bed with various problems. Ben remembered that the boy seemed lonely and could sometimes be seen at his bedroom window, watching the other boys in the neighbourhood play.

I'm usually very sceptical about this sort of thing but I began to wonder of it was the spirit of the dead boy that was writing on my computer.

Back in the house I went up to my office and said 'Jimmy, how about you and I become friends?' For a few minutes, nothing happened but then the computer flashed slightly and went back to read 'Get back to work!' I laughed as it felt like a joke.

Since that day I've had a relationship of sorts with Jimmy. As I work I talk to him about what I'm up to. He hides things, still sometimes will knock a cup of coffee over on my papers if I haven't entertained him enough that day and so we rub along. I can't imagine me ever leaving this house. Any new owners would certainly get a shock if they have a computer.

Melissa, 24

I tried an experiment with my friend Judy recently. She was going to visit a medium and although I would have loved to go with her, work commitments meant I couldn't. I lost my grandmother last year and I missed her terribly and wanted to know that she was OK and wondered if she could still communicate with me.

Judy agreed to ask about my grandmother and late one night I meditated to keep my mind opened and asked grandma to show the medium and Judy a red rose to prove that there was life after death.

I had arranged to have lunch with Judy the day after she had seen the medium. What she told me astonished me. Apparently, the medium kept making notes on paper throughout the session. He told Judy that there was a woman called Rose waving a bunch of flowers and smiling, indicating that she was trying to connect with someone who wasn't in the room but was very close to someone in the room. It had to be for me.

The funny thing is that my grandmother was called Iris, not Rose. Somehow the medium had got the details mixed up. Even though the message wasn't too clear, it had to be my gran answering my plea to show herself to prove that she was OK.

Peter, 53

I have been working as a professional medium for nearly twenty years now. I knew I had the gift when I was about ten years old. I saw my recently departed grandfather standing in a kitchen waving a biscuit tin. When I next visited my grandmother, I looked in the kitchen cupboards and found the exact same tin. Inside was his collection of war medals that was worth a lot of money. No one else had known it was there.

From then on I would often see dead people around my friends and teachers. It was as if they were always trying to get my attention to tell me something. When I was very young I didn't know what to do, I thought perhaps everybody was able to see them.

It was only when I was in college and kept seeing a small child around my roommate that I realised that it was a gift that I had. I don't see ghosts in the sense that most people would understand it, rather I get an image of the deceased person in my mind. They are usually doing something that needs to be interpreted as to what message they are sending. I'm what is known as a clairvoyant.

From the first day I met him, my roommate had a little girl following him. She sat on the rug when he was in bed and appeared whenever he had friends round. Eventually I told him what I could see. His face blanched and he told me that he had had a little sister who had died when he was twelve and she was just six years old.

The little girl was always smiling at him. He said that she had always wanted to come in his room if his friends came round and really looked up to her big brother. I told him that she still did look up to him and was with him most of the time.

As word got around college, people began to come and ask me for readings. I was always able to picture a loved one or family member who had passed and relate any messages. One memorable instance involving my clairvoyant powers happened towards the end of my time in college when I had improved on my skills.

Judy was my girlfriend's best friend and had lost her father to emphysema the previous summer. One night we all went out for dinner and every time I looked at Judy I could see a man with greying hair waving a kite at me. Eventually I told her what I kept seeing and her face looked shocked. She told me that her father loved kite flying, he had even entered competitions flying his kite and when she was a little girl he always took Judy with him.

When she was at home during college vacation she had always gone kite flying with her dad. After I told her this the man in my vision kept showing me a cupboard with a cat calendar hanging on it I related this to Judy and she said, 'Oh, that's the cupboard in the kitchen where he keeps his kites!'

We worked out that her dad was very keen for Judy to take his kites and keep flying them. He didn't like to think of them sitting in the cupboard unused. Judy had since begun entering herself in kite competitions just like her dad had and has thanked me for letting her know that her father is still around.

Most recently I had a sitting with an elderly lady called Sara. I don't usually ask my clients much about themselves so that the information doesn't affect my ability to be open to whatever messages they are sent. When this particular lady came in I instantly felt an overwhelming sadness. As we sat and concentrated, the image of a woman wearing clothes from the 1920s.

She was showing me baby clothes and shaking her head. She was speaking but it wasn't in a language I could understand. I told Sara what I was seeing and her eyes filled with tears.

She told me that her mother, who was Hungarian, had died giving birth to her and not long after her father had remarried and had had another baby, a little girl. From then on Sara was always pushed to the sidelines. While her younger half-sister was dressed beautifully, she was always dressed in rags.

She had spent her childhood on the edge of her family in this way. Her real mother was telling her how sorry she was and how she had watched over her with sadness during this part of her life. Next I saw her mother standing with a man who had very dark brown eyes and a lot of dark unruly curly hair.

He was standing next to Sara's mother and they were both smiling. Sara told me that the man must be her husband who had passed away eighteen months ago. I told her that her mother had been happy for her to have such a wonderful husband and that now both of them were waiting and watching over her in heaven. Sometimes, knowing that your loved ones are with you, even during very hard times, can be a source of great comfort.

Jane, 26

I have a girlfriend called Stacy who is obsessed with numbers. She believes that whenever she sees the number that corresponds with date of the death of a relative that relative is trying to communicate with her. For example, her granddad died on the 21st October and whenever she sees the number 21 she says that it's her granddad with a message for her. Once she got a cab to a party and the fare was $21 so she decided that her granddad wanted her to have a good time at the party and she did. Also she buys things in the sales that are reduced to $21 because she thinks her granddad is telling her she will look nice in it. I think that she's a bit crazy but I have been looking into numerology and it's quite interesting. The numbers of the letters of my name add up to 8 and the apartment I've recently bought is number 8. Maybe that's why I feel so comfortable in it.

Karen, 64

I'm quite obsessed with visiting mediums. I often get feelings that tell me that spirits are trying to talk to me and it is often when I'm at my most confused or vulnerable that I get very strong feelings that there is a presence with me. One particular day I was really feeling like I needed some support and so went to see my medium who I'll call Claire.

Claire told me that there was a man with me and then described my father who had passed away two years earlier. She said that he was always with me and I should feel comforted by this. Then she told me that my father was standing with two little girls and he was indicating that they were my little sisters.

When I was four years old my mother gave birth to twin girls but they died when they were only a few days old. It is such a comfort to know that my little sisters are happy with their father and they're all watching over me.

Kitty, 50

I have always felt that I'm psychic in some way. When I think about any of my relatives who have passed away, I always get a feeling that they are with me still. It wasn't until I was in my mid-thirties however, that I began to take my gift seriously and decided to learn techniques of contacting the dead.

I went to see a medium, David, when I was about thirty-two years old and what he told me proved that it would be worthwhile for me to educate myself about talking to the spiritual realm. During the reading David told me that it was quite difficult for my dead loved ones to make themselves heard, there were many spirits attracted to talking to me because I was so receptive to them.

That night my great-aunt told me that she had also been psychic and I had inherited her gift. She was insistent that I learned how to use it. David began to explain to me how to train your mind to accept the spirit world. One of the most important techniques is meditation to empty your mind of all judgmental thoughts and clear the way for messages from the other side.

As soon as I got home that day I had a long, hot bath and then lit some candles in my bedroom and prepared to meditate. At first it was really difficult I couldn't empty my mind because all kinds of thoughts were popping up.

I tried the breathing technique that David had shown me. Breathe in through your nose slowly to the count of five, breathe out through your mouth to the count of six, and I began to feel more relaxed. As I concentrated I started to feel more relaxed. I closed my eyes and concentrated on my breathing.

Suddenly, I had the sensation that the room had disappeared around me and I felt that I was in a cavern of bright white light. I could no longer hear any noises inside my house and my head became totally clear. I began to hear a sound like glass tinkling and a misty shape appeared in front of me in the white room.

The shape gradually became clearer and it was my father who had died two years earlier, his mother, my grandmother was with him and they were both smiling at me. My grandmother died when I was only four years old and I knew that my father missed her. It was nice to know that they were together again. I didn't try to contact any further spirits that night because I found the whole thing very tiring and needed to rest. I was delighted that for the first time I had made clear contact with the spirit world. It wasn't as detailed or complex as some of the communications I have had since then but it certainly worked!

After a few months I was able to slip into the white cavern very easily and spirits would materialize before me. Most communication was done by showing me things I very rarely hear actual words spoken. I began to do sittings for my friends.

One particular sitting was for Rosie, my oldest friend, who had lost her mother the previous summer. Once I had peacefully entered the cavern Rosie appeared before me. She was showing me a picture of a little white house. When I told Rosie she said that her Aunt Meggie lived in a white house and that she hadn't seen her since her mother's funeral. I told Rosie that her mother was asking her to visit her aunt.

The next time I saw Rosie she told me that she had visited her aunt and was surprised at how dishevelled she seemed. Rosie's mother's death had hit her really hard and she was struggling to keep going day after day. She had never had children of her own and Rosie was now her only surviving relative. Convinced that her mother was worried about her younger sister, Rosie made arrangements to visit her Aunt Meggie regularly to keep her spirits up. I felt proud to have been able to help my friend.

Since then I have found missing heirlooms, prevented a suicide and solved many family riddles. I really do believe that I have a gift and I'm trying to use it for good, to help people.

Damian, 18

I am now 18 years old and I've had the gift of talking to the dead as long as I can remember. I always try to block it out because it actually frightens me a bit. It's because when I was a little boy I only received messages from evil spirits who told me to do bad things that I didn't want to do. I tried to tell my mom but she just laughed at me and told me it was nothing to worry about. I think that she thought it was all in my imagination, but believe me it wasn't.

One of the spirits hated my little brother and was trying to get me to hurt him. I saw him as a large dark man without a face. Whenever he comes through I play music really loud to drown out what he is saying to me.

I have also repeated 'Go away' loudly over and over again to prevent him from speaking to me. I tried to contact a medium so that they could ask the spirit to go away but the medium I saw told me that she couldn't see any dark spirit. Maybe she was a faker because he is definitely there.

Grace, 45

My father died in November 2005. After his death, my husband, our two children and I moved into the home he had shared with my mother who had died two years previously.

When he was alive my dad was such a practical joker. He was always hiding things from you or pouncing on you unawares from behind furniture and doorways. He also used to do simple magic tricks with pennies, making them appear from behind your ear or up his sleeve. Because he was such a larger than life character I really missed him and it was strange being in his house without him. I remember sitting in the kitchen with a cup of coffee, feeling tearful and talking aloud to my dad about how much I missed him.

When I took the coffee to the sink, a penny was lying in the washing up bowl. Not thinking anything of it at the time I put it in the jar we keep on the windowsill for loose change. The next day I was putting on my boots to go outside when I felt something hard in one of them. It was another penny!

Over the first month I found about twenty pennies hidden away and I'm sure it was my dad hiding them because I'd never experienced this before. We tend to use cards instead of cash because it's more convenient. The other thing that happened was that as I went to sleep at night I would often hear a click-click sound. My father had walked with a walker for the last eighteen months of his life and when he walked he sounded just like that noise.

On my birthday I was picking up my presents when I saw a coin on the carpet. It was a sixpence dated 1964, the year I was born. How that got there I don't know because those coins haven't been in use since the 1970's, and we don't have any. My husband agreed with me that it was strange that it had that specific date. On time I even saw a coin come rolling out from under a chair as if just dropped there and then spin round to fall on the floor where I could see it.

There's no one there to drop the coins though. It has to be my dad sending me little signs that he's still with me doesn't it? On his birthday I found a coin dated 1940, the year he was born. It was right there on the drive as I passed.

I take the coins as signs now that my dad is communicating with me. Remembering my birthday and making sure that I don't forget his!

Gita, 48

All the women in my family are spiritually sensitive and have the gift. From being very young I would always have dreams or premonitions in which a loved one who had passed over would warn me of dangers or guide me to make the right choice. When my daughter was born, I knew from an early age that she also had the gift. She was constantly telling me about her conversations with her great grandmother (who passed away before she was born), and could see the spirits of pets after they had died.

My mother also had the gift but it used to frighten her and she never wanted to harness it or develop it. Neither did she help me with my psychic ability, so I always wanted to encourage my daughter to use her powers wisely.

As I talked to her about her experiences, she became more receptive and began having very clear dealings with the spirit world. She has told me about relatives that I haven't thought about in years and like me has premonitions which I always take seriously.

When my daughter was a teenager in high school her

dad (a local fire officer), was working the night shift taking the dispatch calls and I went with him as I occasionally did to keep him company. When he was working the night shift he often switched the phones off during the day so that he could sleep undisturbed. Sometimes he just forgot to switch them back on again.

This particular night I called home but the phone just rang and rang. I didn't think our daughter was out and that the most likely explanation was that the phone was switched off. Just to be sure I tried again about a half hour later and my daughter answered. She told me that the weird thing was that she hadn't heard the phone ring she just knew that she had to answer it. She is very sensitive around telephones and has answered them other times when they didn't ring but she knew someone was calling.

I have also been able to initiate some events just by concentrating my mind to it. When I was a teenager, my mom re-married. Her new husband was a very violent man whom I was terrified of. He often came home drunk and would start a fight that usually ended with mom and me hiding in the bedroom.

Eventually my mom asked him to leave. He stormed out of the house saying that he would be back to 'sort it out'. All night, I prayed that he would never come home again.

That night he still hadn't come home by midnight and when I saw the police at the door, I knew that something bad had happened. He had crashed his car, driving whilst drunk and had been killed. I felt strange because it was almost as if I'd called for his death.

I never told my daughter about that night, but when she was sixteen, the same age that I had been when my mother re-married, she told me that one night when she was home alone, she knew that the phone was ringing even though she couldn't hear it. Thinking that it must be either me or her dad she answered it. She said that all she could hear was the distant sound of static on the line and a man's voice saying 'sorry' very quietly. She thought it was a wrong number but felt that she had to tell me because somewhere in her head she was being told that the message might be for me.

Ever since that night I've felt certain that it was my stepfather on the phone finally apologising for his wrong-doings. I felt so strongly about this that I went to a medium to try and get things clarified further. The reading was quite stunning. The medium described my stepfather in admirable detail and told me about the injuries that had cost him his life.

He told her that he had been coming home to apologise for his actions and that he wanted us to make a fresh start. He said he was sorry through the medium who also said that my great-grandfather had been standing beside my stepfather to show that he did indeed want to make amends.

It was strangely satisfying to know that after all these years, my stepfather can still say sorry to me. I had carried the inner wounds from this period of my life with me for so long that the relief and lightness I felt when I woke up the day after the reading made me feel fabulous.

Jon, 19

My brother Jason died in a swimming accident when he was nine years old. My dad told us that on the day of Jason's funeral he was coming out of the gate to go, and he looked up at his bedroom window and saw him standing there. My brother was smiling and waving at him as if to let his dad know that he was alright.

Jason has tried to communicate with other members of our family too. When my little brother was alive, my Auntie Jill, (my mom's sister), used to visit a lot and every time my brother wanted to get past her, he used to pull her jumper. My Auntie Jill says that she has been in our house and felt her jumper being tugged and then been physically moved out of the way just as Jason used to do when he was alive.

Another way he communicates with us is to jump on the bed. When he was alive, he loved jumping on the bed, especially mom and dad's big bed, and my mom always used to tell him to stop because he would fall and injure himself.

One night my mom and dad both awoke at the same time, and they felt someone was bouncing on the bed, not just lightly but very forcefully as if they was jumping really heavily. My mom's instant reaction was to say 'stop it love, you will hurt yourself' and as soon as she said that the bouncing stopped.

One way or another, the tricks he played on us when he was alive are still being played even though he's now passed away.

Keith, 20

My aunt's husband, Uncle Cory, died during an operation to remove a tumour from his brain. At the time he and my Aunt Kathy had two children, a five-year-old son and a one-year-old daughter.

About two months after his funeral, Aunt Kathy asked Jerome, her son, to watch his sister while she prepared some food. Her daughter Leah was on the sofa asleep but Aunt Kathy worried that she might wake up and roll over and fall on the floor. She went to make some supper and she could see out of the corner of her eye that Jerome wasn't looking after Leah, he was playing with his toy cars on the wooden floor in the hall.

She immediately told him to go back and look after his sister but he kept telling her that it was alright if he played for a while. When she carefully explained why she wanted him to watch the baby he told her tat it was alright because 'Daddy' was in the living room with her.

Then Aunt Kathy looked into the living room at her daughter and saw that her daughter was awake and smiling and gurgling at something just above her.

Her little hands were grasping something in the air but my aunt couldn't see anything. Aunt Kathy was amazed and told us that it really did look like there was someone with her. Jerome insisted that it was his daddy and he could see him. There have been other times when Jerome has told my Aunt Kathy that Daddy was still with them all.

Becky, 38

I have been seeing and communicating with dead spirits since I was a little girl. I am now twenty-four years old and still attract the spirits to me just as I did when I was a little girl. If I enter a hospital it looks and sounds to me like a football stadium. If I wake up in the night the spirits of people who used to live in my house are always standing around my bed trying to tell me things. They are never close friends or family who have passed away they are spirits of people that I never knew.

For the last six months I have been a single mum and we recently moved to a new house. I feel that there are aggressive spirits in the basement of this house and I hear footsteps or things being dropped upon the floor at night.

Friends say that it is just a gift from God and I should try to focus on training my abilities but to be honest with you it scares me.

My youngest daughter is three now and I've seen her do things that I use to do as a child, like stare very intensely at something that I can't see, before she will walk into a room. I have also heard her talking to someone who I can see is not there. When she is old enough I will talk to her about our gift and maybe together we can try to make a little more sense of it all.

Carol, 44

I have been communicating with the dead since I was little. Mostly the spirits I talk to are kind and helpful but there is one man that I'm scared of. I have seen him since I was about six years old and I've always called him the Clown-man. He wears black clothes and holds you down or pushes at your chest so you can't breathe. He makes my bed rattle in the middle of the night and until recently I didn't know what to do about him or how to make him go until recently.

I have just started communicating with a spirit called Mary who says that she is my mother from a previous life. She has started to appear whenever he does and they seem to have some kind of silent fight with each other. I can tell that it is aggressive because of the looks on their faces and the tense energy that I can feel around me. Mary told me that this man was a child murderer. That's why he's now coming for me – because I'm her child and haven't got the full protection from the spirit world.

The last time I saw him, he was standing by my bed in the middle of the night. I felt him touch my face gently and heard him say sorry. The next time Mary came to see me she told me that he wouldn't be visiting me again because he has seen the error of his ways and his spirit is trying to get redeemed by God.

Cassandra, 22

My grandmother died in 2008 from an aggressive form of cancer. From diagnosis to death took only a few months and we were all shaken to see her decline so rapidly. After her death my mother went to stay with my grandfather for a while to help him out with cooking and cleaning because my grandmother had taken care of everything for him.

While she was staying with granddad she had a strange phone call from her brother asking her to come and see him urgently. He lived close by so she told my grandfather where she was going and went to my Uncle Jeff's house. When she got there she found Uncle Jeff in quite a state. He told her that there was a message from grandma on his answering machine.

At first my mom was incredulous. Grandma had died a few weeks earlier, it couldn't be her. Uncle Jeff made her sit and listen to the message. My mom said that at first, all she could hear was static but then a strange voice almost singing seemed to come through the white noise. It sounded exactly like my grandmother.

My mom and Uncle Jeff decided that it must be proof that grandma was no longer in pain and was singing because she was happy. She always sang when she was happy.

Jill, 40

All my family have the gift so it was no surprise that after the death of my mother in 2005, both my sisters had communication from her. She told the both of them that she was now happy and free of pain and that was a great comfort to them.

She used to be quite a large woman but in the weeks before her death her weight had dropped to about 90 lbs. When I heard that she had communicated with them, I felt quite miserable because she hadn't attempted to communicate with me. It's selfish, I know, but it made me feel excluded.

A year later, on the anniversary of her death I was alone in my house and said out loud to her. 'Mum, I miss you please say something to me'. Nothing seemed to happen at first and I took some laundry upstairs to my bedroom. I keep prayer cards slotted around my dressing table mirror and down the left side are all the prayer cards given to me by my mother. When I entered the bedroom however, all the prayer cars were lying on my bed. I hadn't moved them and no one else had been in the house. I put them back all the time telling my mother how much I loved and missed her and that if that was a sign from her then she should give me another one to prove it.

I went downstairs to get some more laundry and once again when I entered my bedroom, all the cards were on the bed. Suddenly I knew it had to be her. One of the cards in particular caught my eye. It had landed a little way from the others and looked to be standing up. I picked it up and read it. 'But the child's mother said, "As surely as the Lord lives and as you live, I will not leave you."'

I truly believe now that my mother contacted me from heaven and that the message proved that she is still with me always.

Gelda, 49

I am a medium and have had the gift of being able to hear the dead all my life. Whenever a spirit contacts me, I am able to feel and visualise the moment and cause of their death. The other night I woke up with the feeling that I was trying to stay alive. I was fighting with a man who had his hands wrapped around my throat. Because of her sudden death the woman hadn't been able to say goodbye to her two young sons and wanted someone to tell them.

I have another woman's spirit trying to contact me. She was stabbed to death by a horrible man with rotting teeth and long, greasy, grey hair. She begs him to stop but he always says that he can't and it has to be this way. The man throws the woman's body into a lake. I don't recognise the lake so there is no point me telling the police.

The other most frequent spirit to contact me is a woman of about thirty years old. She is in her kitchen having a fight with her husband who is about the same age.

Suddenly he pulls a knife out of the drawer and stabs her. I feel the knife and the weakness as the woman bleeds to death.

This woman contacts me every day but I don't know who I should tell about it. Some of the random spirits that try to contact me are not yet on the other side but in a grey area because they didn't die naturally. They come to me for help because although they can see the light they don't move towards it because their death was so sudden and unexpected. Many of them don't even know that they had died. They are just wandering around in a fog of confusion, really. They talk to me because I can hear them, but I don't always know that there is anything I can do. However, I do my best to help them move on.

Sometimes I have been able to contact the deceased relatives of my clients and reassure them that their loved ones are now happy and free from pain. Some spirits contact me to tie up unfinished business or because they want justice in some form. I do my best to listen and pass on their information and it is good to help clarify things for those left behind. Being a medium is largely the ability to listen.

Lola, 58

I have seen spirits since I was a little girl and have also had contact during dreams. I have been able to communicate with many deceased loved ones. I can remember seeing spirits from my earliest memories but it wasn't until my grandfather passed away that my gift became more of a solid reality.

My grandmother divorced my grandfather and re-married and it was her second husband that I was closest to because he was around most of my childhood. I did, however, see my real grandfather, my mum's father. He had a dog that I would walk with him at weekends.

He died when I was twelve and the very night he died I awoke to find him standing in my bedroom by my bed. He told me that he'd come to say goodbye and smiled then disappeared. I only learnt in the morning that he had passed away in the night.

In July 2000, my grandfather appeared to me once more and warned me about hard times to come. He told me to be strong for my family. Several times over the next few months I would have the sensation of someone standing behind me and look around to catch I glimpse of my grandfather.

About four months after my grandfather's warning my brother became seriously ill. The prognosis was that even if he survived his health would be affected for the rest of his life. My brother died on 1st May 2001. He weighed only 105 lbs when he passed. The nurses in the hospital had a ritual that they performed whenever someone died. They would prop the doors open to let the spirit out. My mum and I stood by my brother's bed as they opened the doors and I saw him walk out. He turned and smiled at me and I was amazed because he was back to his normal healthy self, nothing like the emaciated body on the bed.

Over the next few years my brother came back to visit me often. Mostly I could just feel his energy around me or catch him entering the room out of the corner of my eye. At one point, when my niece was pregnant, he told me that she would have a baby girl and she did. He also told me that my grandmother was going to pass away two days before she died.

I have spoken to my mum about it and he has never appeared to her. I think he's worried that it may upset her. She was devastated after his sudden death. Spirits only contact you if you are receptive to them. They don't want to frighten you.

Nancy, 62

Our local spiritualist church invited a psychic to give readings to the congregation. She pointed to one woman and said that she could see lilies. The woman replied that she plants lilies near her father's grave because they were his favourite flower.

She then indicated another woman and said that she could see a toddler playing with toys. The woman's eyes filled with tears and she told her that her son had died when he was just two years old.

A man was told that he had rock pools all around him, his son had died in a diving accident. It was fascinating how accurate the psychic's readings were. I had always been sceptical but after attending that session at my church I have started to believe.

Claire, 29

In 2004 when I was pregnant with my second child I saw my eighteen-month-old begin to chatter away as if someone was there. What was strange was the fact that she seemed to be talking to someone called Jimmy. We didn't know anyone called Jimmy so I didn't know who it could be.

When my husband got home from work we decided to watch a film together after I had put our daughter to bed. At the time we lived in a tiny two bedroom house and the street was fairly quiet. About five minutes into the film we heard a loud crash. At first we were worried that it might be someone trying to break in and we rushed to investigate. We went to our daughter's room to make sure she was OK. She was still sleeping but a picture on her wall had fallen onto the floor. It wasn't broken it just seemed to have jumped off the picture hook and dropped onto the carpet. Our daughter didn't seem to know anything about it and we all carried on as normal.

Several months later, after my son was born, I went to visit my paternal grandmother. I never met my grandfather because he died when my dad was a child. No one ever mentioned him because it upset my grandmother so much. I didn't even know what he was called. I was telling her the story of my daughter and 'Jimmy' when a strange look came over her face. She told me that my grandfather's name had been Jimmy. Apparently his real name was James but everyone called him Jimmy. I couldn't see any way that my daughter would be saying his name if she wasn't in contact with him from the other side.

Katy, 32

My husband and many of my close friends are convinced that I'm psychic. The day before my grandma had a stroke I saw my grandfather in a vision and he told me that my grandma's health is not good. It was as if he had been trying to prepare me for it.

Before I met my husband I worked as a chambermaid in a hotel. There was one room that I always had a strange experience in. A man's wife had committed suicide there after finding out that her husband had been having an affair. Whenever I cleaned this room I would get the feeling that someone was watching me. I would always prop the door open with a bucket and try to do that room as quickly as I could.

One day the atmosphere in the room felt particularly bad. Suddenly the bucket slipped away from the door and the door slammed shut. I immediately got a sensation that someone had grabbed my arm and I heard a voice that said, 'I need to be left alone'. I was quite scared and grabbed my bucket and cleaning stuff and ran down to the reception area.

I told the receptionist what had happened and she said 'Oh, that's really strange. When the woman killed herself the last thing she was heard to say was in a call to room service'. When asked if she needed anything she apparently told the maid that she needed to be left alone. I also learned that that day was the anniversary of her death.

Carol, 27

I began seeing spirits when I was four years old. Back then they were just shadows and I don't remember them saying anything to me. When I was eight years old my cousin, who was six years old at the time, died and at first I could sense him around me but by the time I was eleven I could see him clearly as he came walking towards me. He seemed to be telling me not to be afraid of him and reassuring me that he was alright.

I am now twenty-seven years old and married with a six-year-old son who seems to have inherited my gift. He has told me that there are people dressed in white in his room but that he's not afraid of them because they are friendly. I have no idea who they may be.

Brett, 19

My mum's brother, my Uncle Ed, died before I was born so I never got a chance to know him. My mother has always told me that I am very like him and that we would have got on well if we had met. Like me he was very into music and had many tapes, records and CDs that I eventually inherited.

However, no matter how many times I tidy my CDs they keep getting all jumbled up again. If I've been playing one CD, I'll come home to find a different one on top of the pile as if he's telling me what he wants to hear or telling me that he wants me to listen to something.

I've told my mother and she says that was exactly the sort of thing that he would do when he was alive.

Melissa, 31

I am now convinced that I have psychic powers. A very dear friend of mine, Jackie, died a few years ago in a motorbike accident. On what would have been her birthday I was feeling very sad when I sensed a presence near me.

I seemed to shrink down into my chair and the light changed. As this was happening I became aware of a shape at the end of the bed. The shape turned into my friend Jackie who told me that she was happy and was still with me in spirit because I was always such fun to be with. She actually took my arm very gently and smiled at me. It was very weird because I could feel everything.

Since that experience I have felt many times that Jackie was around me and leaving me signs to let me know it. I sometimes get some very strange images within my head, be it objects like a porch or a jacket or a horizon - and they are all objects I associate with Jackie or places I have been with her.

I also get very emotional at times, as if there was someone shouting or crying near me. There are also many times when I wake up hearing Jackie's voice in my ears. She's always telling me some sort of gossip just as she used to.

Karen, 17

I have always been able to sense spirits. My best friend Lucy can sense spirits but can't see or hear them. About a month ago I was at her house with my mum (our mums are friends too – strange eh?) when we heard our mums talking about their ability to see spirits. Lucy asked me if I could see spirits and when I said that I could see them and hear them talking to me she asked if I'd go up to her bedroom because she felt that there may be a spirit in there. When I walked into her room I could see a little girl playing in the corner. She told me to tell Lucy that she liked her room and also loved the pink top that she was wearing. Lucy was a bit stunned and I could tell that she probably didn't believe me.

We went outside for a while and then we went back in the house. Immediately I could see a spirit in the dining room and suddenly we both felt light-headed, with stomach aches and had difficulty breathing. We also felt very tearful. The shape of the spirit materialised as a young girl who looked about fourteen years old. I spoke to her and she told me that she had been strangled. I noticed bruised hand marks on her neck and her eyes were red around the edges. After the initial choking sensation the room became very calm and the girl told me that she doesn't suffer any more.

I have no idea who she is and no one else in the family believes me.

Christina, 35

A few weeks ago my best friend, Bella died, very suddenly. She often told me that she was psychic and since I am a believer in life after death I never doubted her.

She always said that if she died first she would come back to see me again. However, I was still surprised when a couple of days after she died she contacted me. I experienced the initial contact as a feeling of firm pressure at the back of my head and pressure from behind my eyes.

I shut my eyes and saw Bella standing in front of me. She showed me pictures mentally, some brown shoes with a necklace in the shoe box. At the time I was helping her

Bella's mother clear out her apartment. When I told her of my vision we looked in her closet and found the necklace, one that had actually belonged to Bella's great-grandmother and was rather lovely. We could easily have just put the shoes and box in the charity pile. Bella has also come to me in dreams and told me that she is happy where she is and that we'll be together as best friends again one day

Annabel, 24

About two years ago, my sister and I were waiting for a visit from our aunt. She was supposed to be with us around noon but by 4pm, she still hadn't shown up. We called her house but there was no answer so all we could do was wait for her. That day was Friday but we heard nothing from her all Saturday and by Sunday we reported her as missing.

One of my friends, Alicia, is psychic and because we were so worried we went to see her. She told me that she could see a large lake with trees surrounding it. Alicia said she got a bad feeling about the whole situation.

Then a voice told Alicia to tell everyone that she loved them. There was only one big lake near our town so I called my mother.

She called the police and reported my aunt as a missing person. Two teenagers found her body two hours later. She was still in her car and had overdosed on painkillers.

From the estimated time of death she had been already dead when Alicia made contact with her, perhaps helping those left behind to have closure on her death. I don't feel angry with her. She had severe depression and had struggled with it all her life. She didn't have children because she didn't want to inflict herself on them, which was why she became so close to me and my sister.

Marianna, 42

I have been practising as a medium now for about ten years. Recently I did a reading for a lady in Scotland where I felt the presence of a man. The man told me that he passed over about eight years ago and told me that his name was Tom. I asked him to give me a sign that the lady with me would recognise and he showed me a fishing net. When I told this lady, she immediately understood. Tom was her father and he had worked as a fisherman. All the details were true. He had passed on in November 2002.

Another memorable reading was from a man who came to me through the spirits. He had three objects to show me. A large fruit cake, a red velvet chair and an overflowing ashtray. During this reading I could actually smell the smoke as if it was wafting right beneath my nose. The lady with me told me that the man was her husband and that he favoured one armchair in their sitting room that was indeed red velvet and he chain-smoked all his life. She had often baked fruit cakes for him which he had for afternoon tea.

Roberta, 34

I get visits from my ex-husband who passed away when I was twenty-four. He died in a car accident (this was ten years ago) but doesn't seem to mind that I've re-married. He used to work from home and when he visits, the printer always switches on by itself. The strange thing is that he only visits me when I'm upset about something. When I see him I always feel very calm as if I can accomplish anything.

I am also occasionally visited by a niece who died four years ago. She tends to turn the lights on and off. She was only six when she passed and loved light switches, especially when it was getting dark when she would switch them on and off in various rhythms. That's why I know that it's her when my lights in my house start playing games or flickering. I sometimes shout out loud for her to stop it and then she does, for that day at least.

Tim, 33

My father died twelve years ago and when his death felt very raw, I decided to visit a medium or psychic to see if I could still communicate with him even though he has passed. While we were on a holiday in England, my mother made the acquaintance of a medium called Mr B. He had been working for a long time as a medium at a psychic society in London.

At the time I had just turned twenty-one and my father would have been fifty-two on his next birthday. It all seemed so sudden and unreal to me and because I couldn't really accept it I decided o try to contact him.

Just before I went to meet with him, my mother and I decided to have afternoon tea. The waiter brought a pot of tea and little plate with cucumber sandwiches on it, really English and quaint. My mother had a sandwich but I told her that I hated cucumber and couldn't eat one. My mother told me that my father had loved cucumber sandwiches, part of his often Anglophile affectation. I jokingly said that when I met Mr B. I would ask Dad to let me know if that was true.

When I met Mr B. later that day, I was surprised to feel that I was actually very nervous. Mr B. himself was very charming and actually quite ordinary, not at all what I was expecting. (I was expecting some kind of Dickensian showman).

He asked me to close my eyes and concentrate on connecting with a loved one who had passed away. He said that he would close his eyes and the person I was trying to contact would make contact with him. At this point he didn't know that I wanted contact with my father. I was still a young man so in general one would have expected him to assume that both my parents were still alive.

Suddenly, Mr B. told me that he could see a man with short dark hair wearing a patterned sweater. I knew for sure that this was my father because he had Fairisle sweaters imported from Scotland, another of his affectations that we used to tease him about. He told me that my father was saying to him that he wanted to say goodbye properly and that he was sorry that he'd had to go so soon and that he would always be with me.

All of these things I had expected from any medium because they know that those are the kind of things that bereaved people want to hear. Then Mr B. began to laugh. He told me that my father was waving a cucumber at him and that he had no idea what that meant, did I? That was so uncanny that I just had to believe it.

Cecile, 52

I have been a working medium since I was nineteen years old. I am now fifty-two so that's a lot of experience under my belt. When the spirits of the dead reveal themselves to me initially they are in the shape they were in when they died. They have wounds or pains that I can see and feel. Some spirits tell me how they died, some show me, it often depends on the personality they had when they were here on earth.

They do this to let the sitter know who they are. Thankfully I only get a fleeting sensation of how they died but I am able to relate their deaths to the sitter. I once had a spirit who couldn't see, I tried to make sense of it and the spirit told me that they had lost their head. It turned out to be someone who lost their head in a motorcycle accident. Another spirit waved a useless arm at me. Their arm had got stuck in some industrial machinery and they had subsequently died from their injuries. After I have established an identity the spirit becomes their normal healthy self as they were when they were alive and well in this world.

After we have established who they are, I start getting messages from them. The thing about the spirit world is that they often have lots of things to tell me, not always for the person present at the sitting. They sometimes have messages for friends and relatives of the person present, not just for them.

Sometimes the sitters get confused. I once gave a reading for a woman whose father had died. As well as her father, her son's best friend who had died in an accident at sea came through with messages for her son. She was puzzled because she hadn't known the boy very well.

I pointed out to her that it didn't matter. This boy had things to tell her son and she was one of the best bets to get that information to him. You can't rely on there being too much regulation with the spirit world when you try to make contact. Making the connection is always a bit hit and miss.

Sometimes, once you have connected with a spirit it can be hard to get rid of them. This is often true of spirits who have died suddenly. They may not be sure that they are really dead yet. You need to give them a little guidance to go fully over to the other side. Some mediums get worried about the clingy spirits, believing them to all be bad but I haven't found it so.

There have been some spirits whose energy I have really enjoyed and this is always a positive thing for me. I don't let them linger more than a couple of hours though. Even mediums have to shut out the dead sometimes so that they can have a bit of peace. I usually just tell the spirits to leave but let them know that I'm happy to speak with them again.

One such spirit is a man called Gerald. He was a very well read and well educated man who died at the age of sixty from throat cancer. When his widow came to see me he was eager to talk with her about all his intellectual pursuits on the other side. She was delighted that he was still learning and when his widow left I chatted with him for about two hours. He told me that the spirit world offers answers to many questions that are unanswered here on Earth but he wouldn't tell me what they are. He said no one would believe me.

When someone gets messages from multiple spirits, they often come back to me and that means that I can stay in touch with some spirits for a long time and really get to know them just as I would in this world. Sometimes a spirit never returns to communicate but this is usually because they've said all the things they need to say and want time to get used to their new surroundings. Some people react in a quite hostile way when I tell them what I do for a living but I just ignore them because most people that I've done readings for have always been so grateful to me for being able to contact their loved ones.

Rachel, 23

My closest friend, Sara, died suddenly last year from a severe asthma attack. Like me she was only twenty-two years old and I was so shocked by it. The day before her death she was round at my house and we were laughing over a boy that wanted to date her and who she often hid from when he called because she didn't want to go out with him.

I started having vivid dreams about her from the day after she died. In the dream I'm always trying to resuscitate her, I succeed but when she regains consciousness she is someone else, not my friend Sara.

Then Sara (the true, real one), appears, to tell me to leave the body alone because it's not hers. About a month after her death, Sara came to me in a dream with a calendar. There was a circle on the calendar around the date of her birthday that was two weeks away. I had this dream for five nights straight and decided that on her birthday I would visit a spot on the edge of the woods where we always used to sit and gossip

Her birthday fell at the end of July and it was quite a hot evening as I made my way to the edge of the woods.

I was a little nervous when I sat on the grass. I hadn't told anyone where I was going to be. The sky was darkening and I sat quietly for a while waiting. When the sun had gone down I asked Sara to come and see me. At first nothing happened but then suddenly I was freezing cold and felt very sleepy.

I must have fallen asleep because the next thing I knew, Sara was sitting beside me smiling. She told me that she had always known that she would die young and that it didn't come as a surprise to her. I told her that I missed her and she gave me a necklace with a dove on it and told me that whenever I missed her I should hold the pendant. When I woke up it was completely dark and I didn't have the pendant. However, when I went back home I found her rabbit pendant on the floor of my room.

I sometimes sit in my room talking and gossiping with Sara now just as we used to. If I hold the pendant I can hear her talking to me and making me laugh. She's still the closest friend I have had.

Ellen, 29

My little boy Wolfgang was killed by a drugged driver when he was only five years old. It was just before Christmas and we had been walking back from his school Christmas Carol service. Ever since his accident, Christmas has been very hard for us all.

During the Christmas just after he died I had some

weird experiences. As usual I went with my husband to mass on Christmas Eve. As we sat in church waiting for the service to start, I started to feel very chilly.

I asked my husband if he was cold but he said no and the door was closed against the weather. Then I felt the seat next to me get warm until it felt as if it was glowing. There was nobody sitting there but I got the impression that Wolfgang was sitting next to me.

About a year later I was pregnant again and went to see a medium. She told me that the child I was carrying was a sister to a little boy that was waving at her from the other side. She told me that the sister would always have an awareness of her older brother even though he was no longer of this world.

My daughter is now seven and she has a teddy bear that she calls Wolfgang, she did this long before I could tell her about the real Wolfgang that was the name for him that she chose herself. She often tells me 'Wolfgang said this, Wolfgang said that', as if he were still with us. I hear her chattering away in her bedroom sometimes and feel sure that she is talking to the brother that she never knew.

Marlene, 48

I am a psychic who does readings about once a month. I have had these powers since my earliest memories, my mother and grandmother had them too. One of my most memorable readings was for a woman whose son had died from a heroin overdose. She was very upset because he had been having treatment for his addiction and he was supposedly in recovery. Both she and the boy's father were stunned that he had died because they both thought that he was getting better and that the worst was over.

During the reading the son came through and told me how very sorry he was for what had happened. He had taken heroin with an old friend for 'one last time' and because he had been off it for some months ended up taking too much and dying.

He asked me to tell his parents that he wanted them to try to help others in his situation because there are many deaths of this kind where an addict takes too much after being clean for some time.

The parents of that boy now travel around rehab centres, spreading the word about what happened to their son and asking addicts to think before taking drugs, especially if they haven't taken them for a while. Just as tolerance increases for the drug the deeper the addiction gets so you have to take more, the same is true in reverse. After months sober even a normal dose can kill you.

The boy's parents have kept in touch with me and are grateful that they were given a chance to try to make a positive outcome out of such a tragedy.

Jason, 24

I have always been aware that I have unusual psychic powers. I hear voices in silence. I can't explain it properly but recently I read an article about white noise or electric voice phenomenon. As soon as I read this article, I knew that I'd discovered exactly what has been happening to me throughout my life.

When I was a little girl we had a very old fashioned radio. Because of the remote area in which we lived we often couldn't get the radio to tune in properly and there would be a lot of scratchy sounding noise where I could always hear voices.

At first I just assumed that it was the voices of the radio presenters but they couldn't be heard clearly because of the reception. When I listened carefully to the voices however, they were saying strange things. One was a man's voice saying 'Don't go into the basement' with another man's voice saying 'No, no, it's already happened'. This would be repeated endlessly, it couldn't possibly have been radio presenters.

Sometime later, when I was in college I had a similar experience with the small portable TV that my parents had bought me. Some channels were fine but others would remain untuned and I would hear voices. This time though it was the voices of the deceased loved ones of the people around me. The first time I realised this was one evening when I was eating pizza with my room mate. I could hear voices telling me that Al, my room mate had a message from his 'Uncle Bod'.

It was a strange name but I mentioned what I could hear and he went pale. He told me that his father's youngest brother was killed when he was only twenty-five. He was a keen weightlifter and worked out a lot so they used to call him 'Bod'. His real name was Charles. Al had never told me anything about him so it was weird that I should get that name.

Uncle Bod was telling Al to go home for the weekend. He did and was very glad because his father had a heart attack while his mother was out shopping. There was no one else in the house and his father may well have died if he had been alone.

I've also been given messages from microwaves, answer phones and computers. In fact, anything that is used with electricity and can generate static. They give me messages for people around me, sometimes even if they are not in the room. Occasionally they are spirits who just want to tell me things about themselves. It's not a frightening thing and I've never encountered a spirit who wanted to cause trouble.

Camelia, 20

When I was seventeen, my 22-year-old brother died very suddenly in an accident. A few days after his funeral, I was at home one night during a particularly strong electrical storm. Suddenly the room was filled with a strange warm yellowish light and I heard my brother saying, 'It's alright Cam, it's alright'.

The next day I told mom about it and she said that for some reason her thoughts were with my brother during the storm also. I have had other little bits of communication from my brother over the years and strangely it is always during electrical storms. I know he is OK because he has told me that he is. The few moments when he comes to me are always brief but warm.

Helena, 23

My grandmother has lived with us for a while. She has her own annex that my dad built with her own front door and bathroom and kitchen. One day my mum went to visit her but couldn't get any answer when she knocked on her door. Grandma has walking difficulties so we knew that she hadn't gone out. My mum got my dad to break the door down and we found my grandmother passed out in the bathroom. We called an ambulance and she was taken into hospital.

In hospital she was diagnosed with Alzheimer's disease. My dad said that when he had spoken to her recently she did appear confused. She started to talk about things that had happened decades ago as if they only happened yesterday and kept asking where my grandfather, her husband was even though he died five years earlier.

She was eventually taken into a long term care centre, and we drew up a rota to visit her. The funny thing is, she carried on talking about my grandfather as if he was with her. Also, the things she talked with him about were things that occurred in the present.

One afternoon, she told me that granddad had told her that I had a new bike to get to work on. I had only got the bike that very morning so she couldn't have known that I had it. She said similar things to mum and dad about shopping that mum had been doing and how late dad had worked one night. We could only assume that she was somehow in contact with her deceased husband.

Over the next year her condition deteriorated and she died, but until her death she continued to be kept informed as to what the rest of the family were up to. She died after spending about ten months in the care centre. She had a smile on her face when she died in her sleep. She's probably with granddad now.

Belinda, 56

I have psychic channelling abilities and I've been able to connect with the spiritual world since I was a small child. My parents were always asking me why I spent so much time talking to myself but I wasn't talking to myself. I was talking to real spirits with real names.

When a spirit comes through to me I often get a headache or a pain in my chest and my breathing becomes quite laboured. I often feel their emotions very powerfully. Sometimes I get a feeling of overwhelming anger or of fear but more often there is a feeling of happiness and peace. To connect fully with any of these spirits, I have to meditate to put myself in a receptive state of mind. I need to be in a special frame of mind to find out who's sending me these feelings and what messages they have for me.

I am clairvoyant as well as clairaudient and sometimes can actually see a shadowy figure of who I'm talking to. Other times I just hear them. I travel to different people's houses to get more of a feel for the person they are trying to connect to on the other side. Last year I was doing a reading for an elderly lady whose husband had passed away eighteen months earlier. She missed him very much and wanted to try to connect with him again.

As I went into my meditation I saw a shadow of an elderly man sitting in the arm chair by the window. He was wearing a dark blue cardigan and had small wire rimmed glasses on the end of his nose. I gave the lady a description of what I could see and she smiled and said 'Yes, that's Ed!'

He told me that he still loved his wife very much and they would be together again one day. He complained about his garden, (she hadn't felt up to sorting it out since his death but it had been his pride and joy). She smiled and said that she'd get some help and make sure the garden was in the best state possible come spring so that he could visit it.

I'm comfortable now with my gift, once I learned how to use it, it has stopped scaring and confusing me.

Julia, 35

Last year I moved to a new house in a different town and from the day I moved in strange things started to happen. Whenever I am in bed I get a tight feeling in my chest. I've been to the doctor to get checked out in case it's anything serious but he did lots of tests and they found nothing wrong.

Then the sink in my basement began to flood. I called the plumber but he couldn't work out why it was flooding. The pipes were OK and there were no blockages. They cleared up the mess from the sink and then left. The next morning the basement floor was flooded but it hadn't come from the sink. It seemed to be coming from the walls. Later in the day, my light bulbs began blowing. I presumed it was being caused by the flooding and damp problems but when I called the electricians round they couldn't find anything of concern with the wiring.

That night as I looked in the mirror in my bedroom, I saw a woman standing behind me. There was no expression on her face, she was just staring blankly. I wasn't frightened, she wasn't at all scary.

After that I saw her on other occasions standing by my bed. She began smiling at me when she saw me, and pointed to a cat that was with her. I'd never seen the cat before but after that it was the woman and the cat that appeared to me at night.

Eventually I asked a medium to come round to try and discover what was going on in my house. The medium asked the woman to come to her in spirit and the woman came through to her. She told us that her name was Lily and she had died in the house a long time ago.

She had a cat who she loved very much and because she died before her cat she began coming back to visit him. The cat died soon after her and he came to the house to visit her also, so the pair of them stayed on there together. The medium helped her to be with her cat in the spirit realm and since that day I've never seen either of them.

Daisy, 53

I am a home nurse and I used to look after a lady called Miriam, who had worked as a medium. Her illness didn't affect her ability to do psychic readings and I attended some of her séances now and then.

I remember one night there were about twenty-five people at the reading, all hoping to get messages from departed loved ones. We sat in the church hall which is where Miriam usually held her meetings and I saw a very strange thing. She sat on the small stage with a jug of water on the table by her chair and just behind her I began to make out the image of a person in the lighting on the stage curtains.

As she gave out more and more readings, the image of the person would change. They'd go from male to female, child to adult and race to race. I realised that I was actually seeing images of the spirits who were coming through to her at the reading. Then I saw my mother looking at me from the changing shapes on the curtain. Miriam said she was making contact with a lady who had passed over about three years earlier and she could feel a pain in her lower abdomen.

My mother had indeed died two years and ten months before that day and she died of ovarian cancer. The message she had for me was to get my father to bring down a black wooden box in the attic. That was all she said. After the reading I mentioned what I had seen to Miriam and she told me that I most probably had clairvoyant skills and could develop them if I wanted.

After the reading I went to my father's house, told him what I'd heard and asked him to go into the loft for a black box. He wasn't convinced that it would be there but went up anyway. When we opened it we saw that it was full of the most exquisite jewellery dating back to the 1800s. It had belonged to her mother and her grandmother.

I haven't sold them, although one or two of the pieces seem to be quite valuable. But they are a link to my mother and her family and I want to keep them for my daughter. I'm very glad that I got the message about them though because my dad was due to move to a smaller apartment two weeks later and until I reminded him he wasn't going to bother emptying the attic because he didn't think that there was anything of value up there.

Nadine, 45

I run a business assisting clients with spiritualism, clairvoyance and past life regression. I have been psychic since I hit puberty and from then on it became my whole life's purpose.

Recently I was on holiday in northern France and while walking down the road began to get a terrible pain in my side. I knew it was a psychic pain rather than a real one because by now I know the difference. I suddenly became aware of flowers lying by the road, usually the sign of a road accident. The name Xavier came to me in my mind. I asked in a local shop and was told that a ten-year-old boy called Xavier had been run down by a car and had died in the street.

One of my oddest cases happened about two years ago. A lady called Corinne asked me to visit her house because she was experiencing a lot of strange things in her house. Ornaments were being knocked over, doors were slamming shut all the time, and both Corinne and her two daughters were quite scared. As I talked with them in their home the television came on, not tuned to a station but running just with the static on the screen.

I got the sense that an entity wanted to talk to me through some form of electronic static. It was this energy that was causing the doors to slam and objects to fall over. As I listened to the static I heard a man's voice talking about people ignoring him in his own home. I asked him who he was and he turned out to be the previous owner who had died in the house at an advanced age.

His family had sold the house after he died but he wanted to stay in it. He was getting angry because the new family in the house weren't talking to him. Even spirits can be grumpy old men.

I eventually persuaded him to go into the light and pass into the afterlife. He wasn't easy to persuade. His voice as I listened to it seemed raspy and I asked him how he died. He told me he'd died of lung cancer. He never came back to the house and all the strange happenings stopped.

Leila, 34

I went to see a medium about three months ago. My friend had recommended this woman Carla, and although none of my loved ones had died recently I was still curious enough to go and find out what she might say. I was amazed at what she told me during the reading.

Firstly, she contacted a great-aunt of mine who had died in early 1990. She always wore this particular brooch, silver with a huge amber stone in it. Carla first began to describe a woman wearing this brooch, it is so distinctive that there was no way she could have known about it. I've certainly never seen one like it since. She even knew how she passed (from complications of pneumonia), because Carla kept coughing and saying she was experiencing breathing difficulties.

Next she made contact with a very dear old friend of mine called Roger, who was killed in a horrific car accident ten years ago. Clara was saying something about bar nuts and for some time I couldn't think what she was talking about until it hit me that Roger had loved going to bars and was obsessed with the quality of the bar nuts available. It was a funny quirk of his that we all used to tease him about. Carla told me that Roger misses being out with the gang but will see us all again one day.

Carla also made contact with my maternal grand-mother, Bess, who passed away in 2008. She told me that she loves me and is still watching over me.

I had always been a bit sceptical of the idea of life after death but now I feel that I now that there is such a thing. There was no way Carla could have known any of the information she was able to give me about people in my life who have passed. Not even my closest friends knew some of the details. I am now a convert to communicating with the dead.

Freddie, 32

One of my closest friends Kieran, died when we were eighteen. We used to love snowboarding together during the winter and when his mother phoned to say that he'd been killed whilst skiing, I was too shocked to even cry at first.

I couldn't believe that he was gone. After his funeral I remember driving home and asking him to give me some sign that he was still with me. It was a dark, late January night and as I was driving, snow began to fall onto the windscreen. Tears came to my eyes as I remembered the fun Kieran and I had had in the snow. The strange thing was that when I pulled into our driveway and got out of the car the sky was completely clear, you could see all the stars and there were no clouds, so where did the snow come from?

The following summer when we went on vacation I saw an advertisement for a clairvoyant specialist and took down the number. I made an appointment to see her the next day. The woman I met lived in a tiny wood framed house with the curtains drawn and a small lamp burning on a table. She asked me to sit down and took my hands in hers. She then asked me if I had recently lost a brother or cousin because she could see a boy about my age trying to come through to her.

It could only have been Kieran. She told me that Kieran was telling me not to be sad any more because he was OK. She said he was showing her some snow and telling her that he was in the snow whenever I went out into it. I wandered around stunned for the rest of the day, because of what she had told me.

I felt him with me again on the morning of my wedding when I was twenty-eight years old. It was early April and where I live spring takes a long time to take hold. The day was bright with blue sky and pale sunshine but when I went to get into the car that was taking me to the church, a tiny flurry of snow fell onto my shoulders. I know that it was Kieran approving of the woman I was marrying.

Leslie, 37

I am psychic but I can't connect with spirits for other people, I just have four different spirits who visit me all the time. I can't see them but they communicate with me through my mind and thoughts. If I ask them questions, they can answer me back. They're not frightening and I don't feel that they mean to do me any real harm but there is one spirit that definitely doesn't like me. He often pushes me from behind when I'm cooking or walking downstairs. He also tries to stop me going into the guest bedroom which he says is his. The door often slams shut and the door sort of sticks so it's difficult to open. Sometimes, if I try to get in he just tells me to go away.

Another of the spirits is a woman who is about my age and told me that she died of breast cancer in this house. I get a feeling of love from her and she is very comforting when I'm having a tough time. The other two spirits are children and play pranks on me by hiding things in unusual places. I have found my shoes inside the washing machine and my make-up in the refrigerator, but I don't really mind them being around me.

Mary, 40

I have been developing my psychic abilities for quite a few years now. About a week ago I was contacted by my best friend's grandfather who called out the name 'Granddad Lewis'. He told me to go and console his family. I had met him once a couple of years earlier and that's how I recognised the voice and the name. When I telephoned my friend Jenny to offer my condolences she couldn't believe it because her grandfather had died just last night. I told her about my experience and she was amazed because he must have contacted me just after he died.

I was also contacted by my cousin just after she was killed in a car wreck. She appeared to me in my living room and said that she'd come to say goodbye because she had to go. My aunt called our house with news of the accident only an hour later and I told her what I'd seen and why I already knew.

I have had quite a few premonitions of the deaths of people I know but also I don't always have those premonitions. I think that some people have more psychic energy than others and it's these people who are able to contact me.

I'm not able to contact the dead once they pass over to the other side. I only get contact just as they die.

Danielle, 19

I have often had experience with spirits of people who have passed away. The house I lived in as a child had many active spirits in it. I remember one time when I was about thirteen and my job was to bring the dirty laundry downstairs from the laundry basket in the bathroom.

As I went into the bathroom I heard a voice saying, 'Don't take it'. I looked behind me and there was a man standing in the hallway. He pointed to the bathroom and repeated that I shouldn't take it. I was scared and went into the bathroom to get away from him. When I looked into the hallway again, he had gone.

I quickly gathered up all the dirty laundry in my arms and went downstairs as quickly as I could. Halfway down I slipped because I was rushing and I fell the rest of the way downstairs and broke my ankle. The man had warned me that something was going to happen if I took the laundry downstairs.

Another time I was helping my dad do the gardening when I saw a girl standing in the middle of the lawn. She said, 'Get him to stop now'. I didn't really understand what she meant. My dad was mowing the lawn and I watched as he got closer to her. I shouted for him to stop but he couldn't hear me over the noise of the lawn mower. When he got to the girl he passed straight through her and immediately the lawnmower stopped working. When my dad bent down to fiddle with it to get it working again. I shouted at him to stop, and as he

134

hesitated and looked at me, it started up again without warning. If he had tried to make it work he could easily have injured his hand badly.

Deanna, 43

I have had many psychic experiences and spirits often come to me in dreams. In one dream I was visited by an elderly woman with extremely long white hair. She led me to a mirror and when I looked into it I saw her face not mine. She then led me outside the room and I was in a strange house that I'd never been in before.

There were lots of brightly coloured paintings on the walls and hand made cushions on the sofas. There was a big fat ginger cat asleep on one of the sofas, and the woman said to me, 'Tell her from Betty that I still love her and look after her'. Suddenly everything went dark and cold and I woke up feeling unsettled.

The next day I mentioned the dream to Kate, my best friend. She said the woman sounded like her grandmother. She showed me a photograph of her grandmother and it looked a lot like the woman in my dream.

When I described the house Kate looked astonished and said that was exactly how her grandmother's house had looked. Her grandmother had died after having a stroke two years earlier. When I asked Kate what her grandma's name was, she told me Betty. Then I told Kate what the lady had said to me in the dream and her eyes filled with tears. She had been very close to her grandma and still missed her very much.

Billie, 20

Last year my group of friends conducted a séance after reading about them in a magazine. A friend of ours, Giles, had been killed earlier in the year when he got swept away whilst swimming in a river after heavy rains. We decided to try to contact his spirit. We covered all the mirrors, opened the windows and lit candles around the room. We then all sat on the floor in a circle holding hands. We knew that it was important not to break the circle so we all agreed that whatever happened we wouldn't let go of each others hands. I acted as medium and asked if Giles wanted to speak to us. I asked his spirit to communicate with us by knocking on the door, one knock for yes and two for no.

Suddenly there was one knock from above us somewhere. I asked if the spirit was Giles and we got one knock again. When I asked the spirit if we could see him we heard two knocks on the door. Jane, one of my group of friends began to cry, but couldn't tell us why. She also began to shiver as if she was very cold and then said that she felt as if something was holding her down making it hard for her to breathe. She said 'I'm drowning, I'm drowning' and we realised that she was feeling how Giles must have felt as he died. I asked him if he was OK now and there was one knock on the door.

We all began asking him questions about the afterlife and by saying yes or no, Giles told us that he was with his grandmother who had died six months before him. We also asked if he could predict the future but he knocked twice for that because he couldn't tell us.

Caroline, 26

My mother has told me that when I was about two years old I would talk to my great-grandfather who had died ten years before I was born. My mother was shocked when I said I was talking to my 'Grampa Bertie'. I also had a friend called Sissy who my mother thinks was the spirit of a little girl she had before me and who only lived for two days. She was called Priscilla.

Now I'm grown up I have spirits warning me before an accident takes place. When something bad is about to happen, a spirit will come through to me and tell me. I have witnessed car accidents that I knew were going to happen. It is quite distressing. I never get told enough in advance to stop anything happening even though I know that something bad is going to happen. Even if I stay home I know when a bad event is going to appear on the news.

Nancy, 46

About a year ago my grandmother's oldest sister was hospitalised after suffering a stroke. She was ninety-three years old and not expected to recover. I went to visit her in the hospital with my grandmother and found 'Auntie Florence', as I called her, barely conscious. She kept repeating the name Violet but we didn't know anyone called Violet and presumed that it must be a side effect of the drugs she was taking. Auntie Florence died about two days after our visit.

A couple of months after the funeral, we decided to do a Ouija board session to try to contact Aunt Flo. I sat around the table with my mother and my sister and her friend. We asked if there were any spirits wanting to contact us and the planchette went to yes. Then we asked who was with us and the planchette spelled out Violet.

I was shocked and I told my mother about Auntie Florence calling for Violet in the hospital. My mother asked the spirit if she had known Florence and the answer was yes. We asked if she knew anyone else in our family and the planchette pointed to yes. We asked Violet how she knew our family and she answered with the words 'Alexa' and 'tea'.

The next time I saw my grandmother I mentioned the Ouija board and how we had contacted Violet. I then asked her who Alexandra was and she reminded me that it was her mother's name. Apparently, my great-grandmother used to run a teashop where she made her own cakes. Her baking was legendary and Violet must have been one of the people who worked there or visited.

Auntie Florence had worked in the teashop for a time but by the time my grandmother was old enough to work she had managed to go to night classes to gain more skills and had worked as a secretary instead of working in the shop. My grandmother vaguely remembered that Florence had a friend from the teashop that she used to go dancing with. That friend had died in the 1930s from breast cancer and we think that might have been Violet.

Tony, 23

Not long after I moved in to my apartment, I woke up one night to see a man in my bedroom pushing at something with his shoulder as if he were trying to break down a door or pull something from around his neck. I immediately put the lamp on but the figure disappeared. This happened again a few nights later and I began to feel as if someone was watching me when I was at home.

The next day I mentioned it to someone at work who said that he had a friend who was a medium and might be able to help me out by finding out if there was a spirit in my house. My work colleague Doug came to my house with the medium, who was called Katarina.

Katarina cleared my kitchen table and put white paper over it. Then we all sat down around the table with a church candle lit in the middle of it and held hands.

Katarina said that we mustn't let go of each others hands during the 'reading' because that was for protection.

Katarina closed her eyes and asked the spirits to contact her. Her voice began to get a bit strange and the table shook from side to side. Then Katarina's voice became angry and she began to shout what seemed like insults in a foreign language. I could hear what sounded like furniture being moved around upstairs and the air in the room was chilled.

Katarina began to shout 'Leave us, leave us now' and the door slammed shut. After that the room felt much calmer and Katarina opened her eyes and told me that the spirit of a man who had hanged himself in my bedroom.

He needed guidance to get to the other side and Katarina told me that she didn't think that he would be coming back. From that night on I had no further problems during the night

Personal Messages

Warnings, notices and help from beyond the grave

Sometimes, people may have just one or two psychic experiences in their life and these may take the form of a warning about danger that must be avoided or instructions as to the deceased person's estate or family.

The accounts in this section are from people who have been given messages or warnings by a spirit that they are connected to, or from those who have been given a message from a spirit in the afterlife about someone who is at the moment here with us on Earth.

Janice, 23

One weekend afternoon I was tidying the kitchen when I saw a man appear in the doorway. It was strange because I wasn't afraid and felt instinctively that the man was here to tell me something. He told me that my mother had been taken ill and I had to go round to her house and get her some help. I don't know why I believed him but I did. However, when I left the house I couldn't see him anywhere.

I went round to my mum's house and when she didn't answer the door I looked in through the window. I could see my mum lying on the floor. I took the spare key from its hiding place under a plant pot and let myself in. I called an ambulance and then sat talking to my mum telling her to hang on and help was on its way. When the paramedics arrived they confirmed what I'd thought. She had had a heart attack. They took her straight to hospital.

My mum recovered and one day when I visited her I told her about the man who had come to my kitchen door to tell me that she was ill. My mum asked me to describe him and she looked quite strange about it. She told me that it was her older brother, my uncle who had died before I was born. From the description that I'd given her my mum was sure that that's who it was. He was still looking out for her from beyond the grave.

Jim, 57

My grandfather died in 1990 and my grandmother only lived eighteen months longer. In the months after their deaths I would occasionally smell my grandma's perfume or my granddad's cigars. In 2002, I had a small melanoma on my left leg and spent two weeks in hospital. About a week after getting home my leg swelled with water retention again and my wound became infected.

For the next few months I had chronic pain whenever I tried to walk any distance. I was given antibiotics and gradually the swelling reduced but I was still in pain.

Then one night I dreamed that my grandparents came to visit and my granddad hugged me and said, 'You'll be alright now son.' When I woke up the next morning I was without pain for the first time in months. My grandparents had always said that they'd look after me and it looks like they're even helping me after they've passed away.

Boris, 18

My mom had a baby boy eight years ago who only lived to the age of four when he died of a heart condition. My mom had me a few years later. One day, when I was about fifteen, I was doing the washing up I caught sight of a shadow in the corner of the room. I thought it was a little boy but when I looked there was nothing there. Over the next few weeks I kept on catching sight of this boy but could never actually see him if I turned to look properly.

Then I woke up one night to find him standing by my bed. He said, 'Be late', then disappeared. The next morning I got up for school as usual and had forgotten the strange experience that I'd had during the night. I got the bus to school as usual and went through the usual boring classes during the day. In my English class I realised that I'd forgotten to bring in my homework and Mr Walsh the teacher made me stay behind for twenty minutes after school. I missed the school bus and walked home. On the route back I saw a lot of blue flashing lights of emergency vehicles. A truck had skidded out of control and hit the school bus. No one died but several people were injured.

When I got home I looked through my parents' old photograph album. My mom doesn't have any pictures of my dead brother on display because it upsets her, but there are some in this album.

The boy who I had kept seeing was exactly like the little boy in mom's photograph album. My brother is looking out for me. I haven't seen him since. His name was Daniel and if I see him again I'll say hello and listen to what he has to say.

Laura, 28

I lost my grandmother a year ago. We were very close and I miss her terribly. I am convinced however, that she is still with me and communicating with me. I've always been the sort of person who loses things all the time, my house keys, handbag, even a cup of coffee!

For the past twelve months whenever I lose something I say 'OK, where is it Gran?' and strangely enough I always find it immediately. In the past, things I lost would stay missing for hours, days or even months so this is a new and fortunate state of affairs.

I like to think of her helping me and it is a great comfort to me to know that she is still here. I keep her photograph with me at all times and talk to her constantly. Some people would think I'm mad, maybe I am but if it helps me to feel like this then why not?

Dave, 28

As a little boy I had a great-grandfather who I adored and who I'm sure adored me just as much. I remember him telling me that he would always look after me no matter what happened. I don't remember this incident but my mother has told it to me many times.

She said that a couple of months after he died I was skateboarding up and down the street when my skate-board's wheels skidded off the sidewalk into the path of an oncoming car.

Apparently, my skateboard seemed to lift itself off the ground and deposit me safely back on the sidewalk as if it were glued to my feet. There were several neighbours who witnessed this event and they all said it was incredibly lucky that I didn't come to any harm.

My mother always insists that it was my great-grandfather looking out for me.

Lizzie, 58

I once attended a séance and was shown into a darkened room where people were sitting in a circle. The man who was in charge of the séance stood in the middle of the circle with his eyes shut, asking spirits to contact him.

As I watched, the shape of another person seemed to surround the host, I felt instantly amazed as it became a clear image of my recently departed mother.

She smiled at me and through the medium told me not to be unhappy and that she was happy and in a good place. She also warned me about my old gas fire. True enough when I went home I could smell gas.

I called an engineer who told me that he was amazed I had escaped without an accident. Apparently even turning on a light switch on could possibly have caused and explosion.

I'm glad to know that my mother is OK and that she continues to look after me from beyond the grave.

Colin, 52

I died on the operating table a few years ago. I was having a minor operation, but there were some complications and I lost a lot of blood. At one point my heart stopped and the surgeons had to shock my heart into restarting.

Of course I was unconscious at the time. But when I woke up after the operation, I clearly remembered the moment when my heart had stopped. I had found myself standing near the door of the operating theatre, watching the surgeons gathered around me. The heart monitor was making a droning noise and they were clearing the table in order to apply the plates.

I looked around and my father was standing next to me. He died when I was forty, and I was delighted to see him. He put a hand on my shoulder and smiled. But he told me he didn't want me to stay with him, I had to stay and look after my kids.

He never met my children (a boy and a girl), so I realised he must have been watching us from wherever he was. He put up a hand to say goodbye just as I got dragged back into my body and my heart started beating.

It makes me happy to know he is there thinking of us. And I expect that when my time really does finally come he will be there waiting for me.

I like to imagine we will be able to go off to some celestial pub and have a beer and a chat to catch up on everything that has happened since he went away.

Carol, 35

When I was about six years old I had a bedroom up in the attic of the house that was furnished with old furniture including an old wooden rocking chair that had been in the family forever. My dad repainted it to match the décor in my bedroom.

I remember I once awoke in the early hours of the morning and saw an old lady sitting in the chair, smiling at me.

I wasn't at all scared of her and she told me that she was pleased how well I was doing at school. She also mentioned the names of a couple of the friends that I played with. I eventually went back to sleep feeling very loved.

The next morning I told my mother about it and she said it was probably just a dream but I was really sure it had happened.

However, she did also say that it might have been my grandmother, who died when I was a baby. Apparently she was very attached to me, and was always grateful she had been able to spend a little bit of time with me before her time came.

To this day I believe she is with me. I have seen her a couple of times since then and she always gives me advice. It's nice to have a lost family member be still with you.

Abigail, 30

I have had a lot of different spiritual experiences throughout my life but have only recently started trying to make sense of them. Quite recently I decide to experiment and try to contact my brother who passed about eighteen months ago.

I surrounded myself with white like they tell you to on those TV programmes and said my brothers name out loud. 'William'. I concentrated hard with my eyes shut and suddenly saw these amazingly bright colours.

I heard my brother's voice calling my name. He told me that he was watching over me and that he liked the colour I had painted my front door. (I painted it red about a month ago). Ever since that night I can hear my brother talking to me.

He doesn't always send positive messages though. He sometimes complains and tells me when he doesn't like something. Recently I bought a new car that he didn't like. He kept telling me it was a bad car and that I should get rid of it. To be fair, I found out later at a check-up at the garage that the brake fluid was leaking dangerously, so perhaps it was intended as a warning.

I do now take some notice of what William says to me, good or bad. But mostly I just feel blessed to have the knowledge that his spirit survived after his body died.

Julia, 36

One of the weirdest experiences I've ever had happened in 1987. I was at home watching television with my husband when I very suddenly began to get very sharp and painful stabbing pains in my chest. It got so bad that I was considering calling an ambulance but then the pain stopped as suddenly as it began and I felt peaceful and calm. About an hour later the phone rang and I was given some terrible news. My sister had been found dead in the street.

She had been stabbed several times in her chest as she walked home from an evening out. It seems incredible but she must have been stabbed at the same time as I was experiencing the chest pains.

The calm feeling I got when they stopped must have been when she passed away. At least I knew that her pain had stopped. Her murderer was caught and given a life sentence, though there is no punishment that will bring my sister back for me.

Josie, 31

I've always believed that you can communicate with the dead. As a little girl I was very, very close to my grandmother who looked after me most of the time when my parents were at work. My grandmother died in 1991 and I talk with her often. When she's around me I often feel this by the clues she provides me with.

The symbol of the star is significant between us. When I was a little girl we often went out into the yard to look at the stars and I drew her a picture of a star that I know she kept because it was in her dresser when my mother and I cleared out her house after she died.

Whenever she is contacting me I receive an unmistakable series of star imagery. I remember one week when a friend sent me a silk scarf with stars all over it, another friend made me a card of foil confetti stars and I saw stars in places as diverse as TV, billboards and personalized license plates – seriously, the whole week.

That week was an important time for me as I had an interview for a job as a supervisor that I really wanted. I felt that my grandmother was reassuring me and that gave me confidence. I sailed through the interview and got the job. I thanked my grandmother for helping me.

Another time I was in the middle of making an important decision when she kept sending me messages with the thumbs up image. Five times in three days I saw the thumbs up sign on bumper stickers, billboards even on the cover of a magazine at the gas station. At the time I was wondering whether to move house. I'd loved my old house but felt that it might be time to move on. I took the thumbs up symbol as a sign from my grandmother that I would be right to move on.

I moved house and due to wonderful new neighbours got a new social life in the process. It was absolutely the right thing to do. I constantly ask my grandmother for guidance and she always responds. That's how I know that she's still with me, still communicating with me and still helping me out.

Johan, 52

When I was young I worked on the oil rigs in the North Sea. Because I was inexperienced and very young, I had to stay out on the rigs longer than most people to build up my knowledge. We would be out there for about three months at a time.

My mother ran a bar near the harbour. Once when I was on shore leave I found that my mother had a new admirer who was also a rig man. He was infatuated with her. His name was Bill and he was quite a drinker but also a very good-humoured guy. He was the kind of person who was always happy and he was very easy to get along with. When he was in the bar he only had eyes for my mother, it became quite a joke amongst the regulars.

The following year he didn't seem to be around much and we heard a rumour that he had died while out on the rigs. My mother and I couldn't get confirmation of this rumour because we didn't know him that well and so didn't know his friends or family. One night however, Bill came into a bar that I was in, it was late and the bar was about to shut for the night. I was getting ready to leave and instead of ordering a drink, he followed me to the doorway.

As I was chatting to him I told him how nice it was to

see him and told him that we had heard the rumours of his death. Bill just winked at me and told me not to believe everything I heard. I was surprised that he didn't get a quick drink because he had always seemed to love his alcohol. As we walked he asked me how I was and began asking me about my mother. He told me how much he loved her and that it was important that I remember that. We parted ways at the end of the street and that was the last time I ever saw him.

When I told my mum the next day she seemed puzzled. Apparently she had had a similar experience. She told me that Bill had come into her bar and had a long chat with her. He told her that he had loved her for a long time then thanked her for listening to him and left the bar. Both my mum and I thought this was very odd.

Sometime later we heard that Bill really had died. This time a man who knew him confirmed that he had indeed lost his life in an accident. The night both my mother and I thought we talked to him, Bill had been dead for several months. I'm never sure whether my mother and I had had the same dream or if he really did want to communicate with us so much that he came back from the dead to tell us about his love for my mother.

Jane, 59

I lost my 21-year-old son last year. He had been at college away from home when a police officer turned up on my doorstep. I knew right away that it must be to do with my son Rob, I am divorced and a single mother so who else could it be about? Also, I'd had a strange phone call from his roommate who said that Rob had gone out at about five o'clock in the morning the night before and hadn't come back yet.

The police told me that my son had hanged himself that day. I was devastated, he had been depressed but I hadn't realised how badly. I had always been very close to him however, and his death was such a shock.

For a long time I couldn't do anything. I spent such a long time grieving. It was all I could think about. I even seriously considered killing myself just to be with Rob. A friend suggested that I go to see a medium and said that she'd come with me.

We found one on the internet who seemed to be for real and made an appointment to see him. I was very nervous but Damien, the medium, put us at ease immediately. I was amazed at what he could tell me about Rob without me saying anything. He said he could feel a tightening around his neck and asked how Rob had died. When I told him he said that it was Rob showing how he had died. Damien gave me lots of other facts, about holidays abroad, family pets, even friends from childhood.

Through Damien, Rob told me that I shouldn't commit suicide and that wasn't the way I could be with him. I'm not sure how he knew it, but I had indeed considered that once or twice in the dead of night.

He said that I was good at helping others and I should

make use of my skills. I am now training to become a bereavement counsellor. Speaking to Rob with Damien help really helped me to begin to move on. I know now that Rob is still with me.

Suzie, 17

My dead grandfather told me that my boyfriend was going to break up with me. I woke in the night and could see my grandfather standing outside my window. He was pointing at a photograph of me and my ex that I keep on my bedside table then he shook his head. I felt confused as to what he was trying to say but eventually went back to sleep. However, the next day at school Dan (my now ex) told me that he wanted us to break up. We haven't gotten back together and I haven't seen my grandfather since.

Cory, 54

When I was 26, I had an accident at work. I fell off a ladder and banged my head badly. I was in hospital with concussion for three days. The strange thing is that ever since, members of my family who have died come to me in my sleep and warn me of impending disasters. When the tragedy at Chernobyl happened, my great uncle Stan came to me in a dream the night before, showing me pictures of an atomic bomb detonating.

The next day the disaster was all over the news. My grandma warned me of the fire at Bradford football club and the bombing of the aeroplane over Lockerbie was predicted by my grandfather. He showed me people falling from the sky.

On that occasion I actually woke up and asked my girlfriend at the time, how many people had died in the plane crash and she just gave me a funny look and said that there hadn't been a plane crash.

It didn't happen until early evening and even my girlfriend was a bit freaked out that time. I actually find these messages troubling because I can't prevent any of the incidents, I just know that something is going to happen. It must be something to do with my head injury because I never had them before. Maybe it has made me more susceptible to messages from the other side.

Mark, 33

My father used to work on the cruise ships sailing around the Caribbean islands. The ship he used to work on was quite old, kept in service because of its unusual art deco features and large cabins. All the crew knew that the last captain had worked until he was seventy years old because he loved his job and that ship. He died in his sleep in his cabin aboard the ship. That happened in 1977, the year before my father began working as entertainment manager.

Existing crew used to tell him how Captain Holden would send messages to them occasionally Initially my father was sceptical but the rest of the crew just told him to wait and see.

My dad told me the tale of one of the chefs, Dimitri, on board the ship changing the menu. He'd decided that he wanted to modernise the food on offer. It seemed a bit dated, all steaks and fries. He introduced some new fish dishes and starters such as hot brie with cranberries.

The problem was that the clientele on the cruises tend to be those over or near to retiring age and they were not susceptible to changing their eating habits of a life time. Many plates were being sent back untouched and a few grumbles began to be heard. Dimitri insisted that the customers would grow to like it. They didn't. At first small things started to go wrong. The cranberries would suddenly dry up and be unusable or the fish would be clearly too off to use.

As Dimitri persisted he began to find that crockery would break or the refrigerator would suddenly turn itself off. The final straw came one morning when he entered the galley to find that none of the plates or cutlery that had been in the dishwasher overnight had been cleaned. The dishwasher could be turned on but it wouldn't wash.

Dimitri's colleagues were by now telling him to abandon his modernisation programme because it was clear that the old captain didn't like it. Reluctantly he agreed. After he re-ordered more traditional foods the whole galley became serene and in full working order again. That was all he had to do.

Mt father also told me of something that happened during his first cruise after he got the job. He was having particular trouble with a singer who had the attitude of a spoilt diva. She constantly insisted that her room had a bad aura and that she wanted a better room. The problem was that there was no other room available. This woman also took against one of the maids, accusing her of hiding things in her room. Eventually the complaints started to wear my father down.

He told me that one night when he was on deck when he suddenly felt a presence behind him. He turned around but no one was there. A piece of paper on the floor caught his attention. Reaching down he picked it up to realise that it was a newspaper cutting. It was a report from a New York paper detailing how a singer had been sacked from a minor role in a Broadway production after stealing from her colleagues and trying to undermine them on stage.

The singer was none other than the woman he was having such trouble with. Feeling buoyed up he took the newspaper clipping to the woman's room the next day and told her that he now knew her history and would have to let her go if she couldn't find a way of being more pleasant on the ship. Shocked at being exposed the woman agreed to change her attitude and from then on the ship was a more harmonious place to be. My father always believed that the newspaper cutting was brought to his attention somehow by the old captain who was letting him know that he was on his side.

Lily, 18

When I was a little girl, my mother and I lived with my grandmother. She really loved having us live with her and never seemed to mind cleaning up after us or cooking us a meal. She was a very powerful personality. Whenever she entered a room you felt it before you even saw her. She was full of fun, always up to practical jokes.

She also used to tell me that she was psychic and could communicate with people who had passed. She always reassured me that after she died she would stay with me looking after me.

When she died my mother moved towns because she couldn't bear living in the house where we had all been so happy with grandma. It was after we moved in that strange things began to happen. Furniture would move, ornaments would fall off shelves and pictures kept falling off the wall.

I was convinced that it was my grandmother but my mother was more sceptical and put it down to the house moving on its foundations because changes in the weather.

The pranks continued. Over the years I've found icy snow in my boots in the middle of July and sand in my coat pockets. I think that grandma loved looking after us so much that she has decided never to leave us. Whenever it is mum's birthday or mine, the whole house smells of roses – her favourite flower. Things continue to disappear and reappear and the odd ornament ends up on the floor overnight, but it's not scary. It's good that we can have fun with grandma, even after she has passed.

Kirino, 56

My mother and grandmother were always telling me and my sister about the 'family jewels'. This was jewellery that had been passed down in the family and was kept by my mother's older sister, our Aunt Cheiko, who we didn't see very much. When we did visit her she was always grumbling that the only reason she got visitors at all was due to her money. We didn't see much of Cheiko once we were teenagers and we more or less forgot about the jewellery.

In 2001, Aunt Cheiko was the last of her generation in our family. She had never had a family of her own. My mother and grandmother had already passed away by then themselves, so Aunt Cheiko had no direct relatives to inherit her possessions. We vaguely assumed we might get something when she died, but we certainly weren't counting on it.

One day I had a very vivid dream. In my dream a very old woman appeared and asked me to lend her a gold bracelet that had been in my family for centuries. After I had given away the bracelet, my mother appeared warning me about something. In the dream I chased the old woman to get my bracelet back. I understood from my mother that she couldn't help me with this task. I awoke from this dream with my heart pounding.

Two days afterwards, late in the evening, there was a knock on my door and when I opened it I was surprised to see an old woman. She was my Aunt Cheiko's neighbour and had come to tell me that my aunt had died in hospital after a brief illness. She wanted me to give her the spare key to Cheiko's apartment, and gave me a story about how she was worried about the cat.

I thought I knew where the key was but I didn't feel I should just hand it over. I told her that I would bring the key to her the next day. At this she appeared agitated but she eventually went away.

That night I had another dream in which my mother once again warned me that something bad was happening. The next day I found the key to Aunt Cheiko's house and went to the neighbourhood where she lived. When I got there I saw that the window at the side of the house was broken. When I went inside it was clear that her apartment had been burgled. There was no cat, and I don't believe she ever kept one. I immediately called the police.

When the police arrived they called on Aunt Cheiko's neighbours to see if anyone had seen anything. The old woman who had wanted the key said that she hadn't seen anything, but the neighbour on the other side told the police that the old woman's son had been moving things into her apartment. She remembered it because he was doing it in such an urgent hurry. The police searched the old woman's home and found art and other belongings that had been taken from our Aunt's home. They also discovered a velvet bag containing Aunt Cheiko's jewellery.

These were taken as evidence and eventually returned to me and my sister. My mother had been telling me that the old woman did not have good intentions.

Juliette, 24

My friend Cheryl had always been very close to her grandmother, who was known locally for her work baking and decorating celebration cakes. When she died, Cheryl was heart-broken with grief for a long time. She told me of a strange experience she had a few weeks after her grandmother had passed away.

One night she woke up and noticed something near her bedroom door. She told me that she could see her grandmother outside her room in the hallway. Her grandmother told Cheryl that everything was going to be OK, that she was always with her and that she should just lie down and go back to sleep. That weekend Cheryl got the urge to bake a cake.

To her astonishment she managed to bake and decorate a cake as brilliantly as her grandmother had. She said it was the first time that she had ever tried to do it and she thought that her grandmother had passed on her skills to her that night.

Stacy-Jo, 26

My mother died when I was 22. I work as a waitress at the restaurant where I met my boyfriend. He works as a chef there. Next door to the restaurant is a launderette and I often take my clothes there to wash when the restaurant is a bit quiet. One night I had dropped off some clothes and was walking back to work when I felt a hand on my arm. I looked down but couldn't see anything there.

Next I heard my mother's voice saying 'Stop, don't go in there!' Instinctively I hid by the side of the door. What I didn't know at the time was that inside, there was a man holding up the cashier with a gun, demanding money from the till.

The rest of the restaurant staff had been ordered to lie face down on the floor. A few seconds after I paused, he burst out through the doors and ran off down the street. If my mother hadn't told me to stay where I was, I could have got in his way and might have been killed.

Jo, 20

My mother tells me this story occasionally. She still cries when she tells it. My brother, Sammy (her first child), had Downs Syndrome and died at the age of five in 1985. He had a hole in his heart and surgery couldn't help him. Almost two years later, my mother had another baby boy, my brother, Christopher.

One day in 1988, my mother was up in the study in the loft doing some work from home, and my dad was in his workshop in the garage. Christopher, who was one year old at the time, was sleeping in his playpen in the kitchen.

Suddenly, my mother heard Sammy's voice saying, 'Dadda, Dadda' as though he was there next to her in the loft. My dad heard the same words spoken by Sammy out in his workshop. They both were convinced it was Sammy's voice. Dad charged upstairs to tell my mother while at the same time my mother was on her way to tell my dad.

When they reached the kitchen doorway they found my brother Christopher holding a plastic grocery bag over his face. My mother and father immediately took it off him and then puzzled over what had just occurred. They decided that it had been Sammy telling them that my older brother was in danger and they needed to get to him fast. Sammy's voice probably saved Christopher's life.

Eva, 34

This is a story that my mother told me. It happened in the 1960s in Hamburg. When my mother was just fourteen, her father (my grandfather) died while out training. He had been in the armed forces all his life and died very suddenly from a heart attack.

My mother and grandmother were devastated. My grandmother had always relied on him to sort out the family finances and take care of repairs. She knew that he had invested some money years earlier and so thought that she must be entitled to something now that he had passed away. However, when she spoke with their accountant he seemed to be telling her that there was no money for them. My grandmother didn't understand and went home bewildered and very worried about how her and my mother, were going to cope financially.

Back at home very weird things started to happen. There would be noises in the night from creaking floor-boards as if there was someone pacing around at night. Once my mother woke up in the early hours of the morning and could hear a bath being run.

She got up to see why her mother was having a bath at 2am, but the bathroom was empty. My mother's room was right by the bathroom and it was quite loud when anyone ran a bath so she hadn't mistaken the noise. Both my mother and grandmother began to wonder if it was the ghost of my granddad pacing his home at night.

About a month later one of my grandfather's oldest

friends, Ollie from the army, came to visit them. He told my grandmother that he'd had a weird dream in which my grandfather had begged him to go and help my grandmother. My grandmother told Ollie about the investments that hadn't produced any returns and he promised to look into it for them.

He took all the paperwork off my grandmother and began looking through it. He discovered that my grandmother should have around 150,000 deutschmarks in returns from the investments but the accountant had said there was nothing. My grandmother got the police involved and they discovered that the accountant had been stealing from them for about 20 years. He was taking the income for himself.

With Ollie's help, my grandmother hired an attorney and the accountant was convicted of fraud and ordered to pay back the money he had taken. I believe he had to sell his house to do it. The strange thing is that from then on all the weird night-time noises stopped and the house became peaceful again. I think that my grandfather couldn't rest in peace until my mother and grandmother were taken care of financially.

Samira, 24

When I was about ten years old, we moved house for what felt like the tenth time but was actually the fourth or fifth time. I liked the house we moved into and felt at home there from the start. I shared a bedroom with my brother who was nearly twelve and he told me that I had started to talk in my sleep but not the usual sleep talking mumblings. He said that I appeared to be actually having a conversation with someone. I also began to sleepwalk. A few times I woke my brother asking him to come and look at who was in our room. He told me that he never could see anyone there.

One night I do remember from this time, I woke up to see an elderly lady sitting at the bottom of my bed. She looked very happy but I was terrified. I did that typical frightened child thing and put the duvet over my head. Nobody would believe what I'd seen.

Some years later I was visiting a cousin when I saw a picture of the lady I had seen in my bedroom I asked who it was and it turned out to be my great-grandmother. She died before I was even born but everyone always told me how like her I was. That night she came to me in a dream. She told me that she was sorry for frightening me when I was little and that she often enjoyed visiting me because I was so like her. When I woke up the next day I no longer felt confused. My great-grandmother was watching over me and it wasn't at all scary.

Brian, 22

My grandfather was my hero and I was devastated to learn that he'd died suddenly when I was just sixteen years old.

When I turned twenty-one, my cousin (Jessica), was twenty-two and had just found out that she was one month pregnant. She told us that her and her husband had decided to keep the sex of the baby a surprise and asked the nurses not to tell them.

Jessica told me however, that she had had a dream about our grandfather in which he had visited her and asked her what she was going to name her baby girl. She wondered if he was trying to communicate with her from beyond the grave. She had the exact same dream when she was four months pregnant and was asked again what she was going to call her daughter.

She told me that it was very strange because she was telling our grandmother about her dreams when our grandmother said that she had also had a dream in which my grandfather told her that she was to be the great grandmother of a beautiful baby girl. The girl was to be called Lily after our grandfather's mother. Jessica supposed that this was a sign from grandfather about what he wanted and decided that if she had a girl she would call her Lily.

At nearly nine months pregnant Jessica had another dream about our grandfather again. This time he said that she had to wake up because it was time for Lily to enter the world. When she woke up she was in labour and at 3am had a beautiful baby girl. Of course, she called her Lily.

Ralph, 18

I am one of three brothers and when I was thirteen, my father died suddenly. It was devastating for all of us. My mother went out to work and I was given the task of looking after my youngest brother, feeding him, bathing him and getting him ready for bed.

Those weren't very happy days for our family because on top of this, my older brother had been charged with assault after he was attacked by a gang with knives and tried to defend himself. He was being held on remand and his court date was coming up.

On the day of the start of his trial our mother went to court to show support for him and I was left home to take care of Ross, my little brother. I had a strong feeling that my brother was going to prison.

Suddenly his photograph fell off the wall and as I turned around I saw my father open the front door and then shut it again. The cupboard door in the hall did the same thing as did the refrigerator, cooker and living room door. All of the doors opening and closing like cell doors. I think it was my father preparing me for more bad news.

When my mother phoned from the court I already knew the verdict and when she said that my brother was going to prison I told her what had happened and that I already knew.

Jerry, 29

My grandfather Rory died in 2000. He had been receiving treatment for kidney failure for three years before his death and eventually he lost the fight. We saw him in hospital two days before he died and he told us he had no more than a couple of days left. He could tell that he was dying. Because they were so close, we all thought that my grandmother would soon follow him but she proved us wrong and lived for another eight years.

She was diagnosed with cancer in 2008. She decided not to go ahead with chemotherapy because it would ruin her quality of life but couldn't cure her. Grandma lived only five miles down the road from us and we all visited her every day during her illness.

A week before she died I was sitting on her porch with her. Her mind was wandering a bit at that stage because of all the pain medication she was on. Suddenly she turned to me and said, 'You'll never guess who dropped by today'.

She began telling me that my grandfather had called round and told her that he'd come for her soon. He just turned up at the kitchen door and said that he couldn't wait to be with her again. She seemed so happy to see him and told me that she couldn't wait to see him again

About five days later she took a turn for the worse and had to be admitted to hospital. I visited the next day but she was no longer coherent. Grandma died in the early hours of the morning. My mum was with her and told me that just before she died she smiled and waved as if greeting someone. It must have been my grandfather coming to get her just as he said he would.

Tanya, 23

My father died when I was thirteen years old. My mother became a widow and my sister and I were left fatherless. We had to learn to rebuild our family. The real depression hit about six months after he died. It was as if the shock had worn off and we had to finally face the reality that we would never see him again. I didn't even get to say goodbye to him.

As this dawned on us, some strange things began to happen around the house. I started to hear loud knocking on the walls but we lived in a detached house so it couldn't have been the neighbours. They were very loud deliberate knocks not just a banging sound. I told my mom but she didn't believe me until she heard them herself. She told me that she was in her room one night feeling at a very low ebb, when she too heard knocking on the walls of her bedroom. The knocking continued until my mom called out my father's name and asked him to stop. The knocking stopped.

Then the TV would come on all by itself or the channel would change when we were watching it. It just felt as if someone was having a joke with us. There was a room in the basement that my dad used for his sports stuff and his shotguns. Since his death no one had been in that room because we couldn't face it. One night we noticed a light on under the door to this room but none of us had switched it on. I went downstairs with my sister to turn it off.

The strangest thing was that the room was locked and the key was upstairs in the kitchen. When we unlocked the door to switch off the light both my sister and I felt there was a blast of air, as if my father had rushed out of the room. Later when we tried to make sense of it we decided that my father's spirit must have been locked in his room in the basement and he had been trying to get us to let him out.

Bobby, 20

My grandfather died when my mom was only eighteen so I never knew him. I remember waking up one night when I had a bad fever. I must have been about seven years old. There was an old man standing by my bed. He put his hand on my forehead and told me that I was on the mend. When I woke up the next morning, my fever had gone.

I saw him again about a year later when I was on the school bus. The bus stopped for an old man who was walking across the street very, very slowly. I looked out of the window and it was the same man I had seen in my bedroom. He even gave me a smile.

I haven't seen him since then, but I think he was letting me know that he will be there if I really need him.

Gill, 34

Joanna and I were best friends all though school and we stayed in contact throughout college. We even ended up living in the same city after graduation. Somehow, we gradually lost touch after my husband got a job in another state and Joanna got pregnant with her third child and wasn't up to travelling much. About two years ago my husband and I divorced and I moved with our two children to my home town to be near my mother so she could help with childcare.

After I had been living there for a couple of months I had a dream where Joanna came to me and asked me to give her sister a message. She wanted to tell her sister that she was OK with her taking care of her children. I woke up confused about the dream but put it down to all the distress I had been under with the divorce and the house move. A few nights later I had a similar dream but this time Joanna was a little more impatient with me. She insisted that I call her sister.

The next day I entered Joanna's name in an internet search and discovered that she had been killed in a hit and run accident about a year ago.

I telephoned her older sister who I had never met and

she told me about the accident and how she was now looking after Joanna's three children because Joanna's husband had died a year before Joanna herself had been killed.

Her sister was in tears as she told me that she was raising her sister's children and prayed every day that she was doing a good job of it. I told her about the dreams I had had and we decided that it actually was Joanna contacting me from the afterlife. For her sister, my telephoning her was the message that she had been praying for so she knew she was doing the right thing with the children.

Rachel, 22

There is a portrait of my grandmother when she was young, above our fireplace. She died before I was born and that is the only picture of her that I have ever seen. When I was a little girl I used to sit on the rug gazing at her. It really is a beautiful portrait.

My mum told me that after my grandmother died, she and her sister (my Aunt Robin) argued over who would get to keep the painting. Eventually it went with Aunt Robin but my mum told me that she felt a strange sensation in her head as if her mother was shouting at her that she had to keep the painting. It was hers. The night after the painting was taken away my mum said that she saw my grandmother in her bedroom one night.

Grandma had said that she had decided to come back.

The next day Aunt Robin telephoned and said that she had been watching TV at home when the painting of my grandmother suddenly seemed to leap off the wall. It is quite a large and heavy painting that took two men to lift and hang. She had been so shaken with what had happened that she told my mum to come round and get it and bring it home. Now it hangs peacefully above our fireplace.

Julianne, 20

My favourite aunt, Auntie Kelly, died when I was fifteen years old. I took her passing very hard because I was very close to her. She lived with me and my mother for a few years when I was little and she often looked after me when my mother was at work. I didn't really laugh for many months after she died but, later that summer, my class had a camping trip and I was quite excited to be going. I hadn't been excited about much for quite a while.

We all set off on the bus and I sort of dozed for much of the way. I do remember dreaming about my Auntie Kelly and she was telling me that she would be looking out for me. When we arrived at the campsite we got into groups to be allocated our tents and then were given a choice of activities for the next day. My friends and I decided to go hill walking.

We were given a map and directions and set off on our

own on the hill walking exercise. We had been given a packed lunch and when we set off the weather was fine and dry. After about an hour we had got quite far up the hill and the sky began to darken. It was clear that there was about to be some sort of bad storm so we began to walk a little faster.

When it started, the rainfall was very heavy and the ground began to get slippery. Because we were also hurrying we were sliding about a bit too. I suddenly slipped on a steep bit of ground that had become very muddy. I don't know what happened but my ankle twisted so badly I couldn't stand up again. The two friends who were with me tried to help me up but there was no way I could get up and walk with them. We decided that they would go back to camp and get help. I waved them off as they left, trying to look cheerful.

The rain began to come down harder and the ground that I was on started slipping down the hillside. At the bottom was now a fast moving river, swelled by the rainfall. I knew I had to do something or I would end up in the river and drown. I began to pray for help.

Suddenly, I felt hands on my shoulders and someone began to pull me back to the top of the hillside. I heard my Auntie Kelly say, 'It's OK, I've got you, I won't let go.' She helped me to the hilltop and stayed with me. I saw rescuers coming about half an hour later and waved to them. They put me on a special stretcher to take me down to camp. While they were strapping me in I looked round for Auntie Kelly but she was nowhere to be seen.

I asked the rescue crew if there had been anyone else with me but they said that I was alone when they saw me.

I know that my Auntie Kelly is still with me and looking after me and it makes me happier, despite the fact that I still miss her so very much.

Glenys, 68

About eighteen months after my husband died I kept waking up at night because of an intense pain in my right arm. One night I dreamed that I had woken up but my husband was there with me and he told me that he was going to make my arm better. He began massaging my elbow and I remember how warm and soothing his hands felt. The odd thing is that when I woke up in the morning, the pain had gone. It has never come back.

Joyce, 28

As a little girl, I thought the world of my grandfather. He looked after me during the school holidays, teaching me about animals and flowers. He died about ten years ago and in the months leading up to his death he gave me many hints that he knew that his time in this world was coming to an end. He even said that he would see me again in heaven.

I am now twenty-eight and have a daughter of my own who is eight years old. I have a strong feeling that my grandfather is communicating with my little girl by leaving her flowers. She calls him the flower man and has described him quite accurately. She says he is with a lady who fits the description of my grandmother who died five years ago. I have shown her pictures and told her that they are dead. But she seems to think they're people who are alive and who she often sees as she heads for school in the morning.

I would love to think that they know my little girl and that she has been given the gift of being able to communicate with loved ones who have passed away.

Kirsten, 28

My grandmother died in January 2004. My sister and I really missed her. She was very outspoken and she didn't care even if hurt your feelings. About six months after she passed away, my sister and her children, three-year-old Mark and seven-year-old Lindsay came to visit to help my mother who was very upset. Lindsay used to tell us 'Grandma Harriet is getting angry because you all keep sitting in her place at the end of the sofa.'

One night we sat down for some supper and then I washed the dishes while my sister took the children upstairs to my bedroom to put them to bed in the fold out beds. When my sister didn't come downstairs, I went up and found that my sister had fallen asleep on my bed so I decided I would have to sleep on the sofa (It was supposed to be my sister doing that).

I took a blanket and pillow from the linen cupboard and settled down to sleep on the sofa. As I was falling asleep I suddenly heard my grandmother's voice yelling, 'Get your feet off my sofa!' I swear I wasn't dreaming it. The next morning I told my sister what had happened and she looked startled then told me that our grandmother had popped her head round my bedroom door and told her not to let the children sleep in too late or they'd become spoiled.

We had to laugh to think that our grandmother was still grumpy and yelling out orders from the afterlife!

Paul, 17

Last May, my fourteen year old cousin, Sam, died from a drug overdose. There were two other boys with him but they survived. The actual events of that night are quite hazy because no one had seen or heard from them for twelve hours until they were found.

In the weeks after he died, Sam came to me in my dreams and showed me what had happened. He showed me that they had smoked heroin, then drunk some beers. After that they shared out some pills that one of them had brought along. There were quite a few different pills but I've no idea what they were.

Sam told me that he was the first to lose consciousness but the other two had taken so many drugs themselves that they didn't notice him. In my dreams I would always grab on to Sam and shake him telling him to stay with me but he always says 'only this time.'

I can't get him to answer any more of my questions but I have told my story to the police and the district coroner and they say that my version of events is probably quite accurate. Sam's two friends have confirmed that they took heroin, beer and pills that night. I think Sam needed to know that someone was telling the truth about his death.

Graham, 61

My story of communication from the dead is a weird one. Before she died my wife always had her cell phone programmed to sound the ring tone when she needed to take her pills (she was taking medication for diabetes and high blood pressure).

I kept her phone as a memento. I couldn't bring myself to get rid of it. I kept the alarm setting at first because it reminded me of her. It was as if I wanted to feel that she was still there and I was so familiar with the alarm ring tone that the place would feel very quiet without it. I did eventually turn it off but the strange thing is, the alarm still goes off! It is always when I am doing something that I know she would disapprove of like drinking too much or not cooking healthy food and relying on take-outs.

I even asked my son to turn off the alarm in case I was doing it wrong but still the alarm goes off from time to time. The last time was when I had a few friends over and we had some beer and a game of poker. It was funny because the alarm would go off whenever I was about to reveal my cards. Maybe my wife was making sure I didn't lose.

Kelly, 43

A few years ago, I was suffering from really bad depression. My daughter has bipolar disorder and looking after her could be very hard sometimes. I was nearly suicidal but my Aunty Fliss had committed suicide ten years earlier and it had devastated our family. However, one day I really was feeling that things were unbearable and began thinking seriously about killing myself.

I was so tired that I lay down on the sofa and must have fallen asleep. I dreamt that someone was knocking on the door and I went to answer it. There on the doorstep was my Aunty Fliss, she told me that I had to let her in because she had come to help me. She came in and told me that although she was now at peace, she didn't want any more suffering inflicted on her sister (my mother), and that I would get through it. She told me how much all the family loved me

When I woke up, I didn't feel frightened or depressed

any more. I believe that Aunty Fliss was watching over me and wanted to make sure that I didn't do anything stupid. My daughter is now on medication for her bipolar condition and it really makes a big difference. She is also much happier. Fliss was right, it was far better for me to stay here and keep fighting. Life isn't perfect now, but it is a whole lot better.

Colin, 26

My best friend Daniel died a few weeks ago. He had been diagnosed with cancer and from that point his health had deteriorated very quickly. The morning after he had died his wife telephoned me with the sad news. I had known Daniel since school and it was so heartbreaking that his life had been cut so short.

Later that day I had to go to a meeting in the city centre. Before I got on the train I stopped by the post office and collected the mail. While I was on the train I sifted through the mail and found quite a few misdirected letters, meant for a different address. One was a postcard with a picture of a beautiful beach on it. The caption read, 'Having a calm and peaceful time'. There was no writing on the reverse other than the words, 'Love Daniel' written in block capitals. It gave me the strangest feeling. How odd that such a thing should find itself in my mail the day my friend Daniel died.

James, 19

My brother died six years ago from a brain tumour. I can still see his spirit and hear him talking to me clear as anything. Some friends and family members think I'm nuts but my mum believes me.

When I am asleep my brother tells me about things that are going to happen in the future. He helped with my end of year exams at school to make sure I got the grades for college. He always wanted to go to college but sadly he died too young to go. I think that was why he was helping me, going through my revision with me when I was asleep.

I'm now at college and my brother is still speaking to me as if he was here too. He teases me about girls I like or chides me for not working hard enough. My brother did go to college in the end; it was just that he had to wait for me to get here.

Keith, 22

I have always felt that I can connect with spirits and as I got older, after my Uncle James died, I thought I might try to contact him in the afterlife to see if he would come to me. I was very close to him as he was my dad's brother and round our house all the time. His death was viewed as unexplained, and as a possible suicide.

One night recently I turned the lights down and lit a

candle in my living room and sat in a comfortable arm chair. I suddenly became very cold and dizzy and my throat was burning. Then the room started to spin. I realised that the sensation I was feeling was the affects of alcohol. Uncle James had always been a big drinker but no one could work out the extent of his drinking.

He had been found dead in his living room and because he had died a few days before he was found, the cause of death was unsubstantiated. From channelling him I began to realise that he had died of alcohol poisoning. I was worried that he'd committed suicide and asked him out loud why he had done it. At first I got no reply, so I went up to bed.

That night I woke up to see a shape standing in the doorway, as I looked harder I could see a faint shadowy outline of Uncle James. He told me that he was sorry and he hadn't wanted to die, he'd just had a bad day and was drinking to relax. He didn't mean to drink so much. At least I know that he didn't kill himself on purpose.

Alan, 25

One of my friends died in mysterious circumstances a few months ago. He had been decorating at his new house with his girlfriend when he was electrocuted and killed. There are some in our group of friends who didn't like his girlfriend and think that she might have had something to do with his death.

I had a dream the night before his death where I was trying to find him, knowing that if I could find him I would be able to help him somehow, so when I heard that he'd been killed the next day I was utterly shocked.

About two days after he died, he visited me in a dream and told me, 'She took the wires, she took the wires'. I have no idea what he means. The house had just been re-wired and they were due to move in the following week. When police checked the wiring there was no problem with it to explain why my friend died.

Whatever might or might not have happened there isn't any evidence or the police would have found it. She has already moved on and is with another man. Conveniently for her the insurance on the mortgage means that the house is now hers and all paid for. She doesn't seem to miss him very much.

Alberta, 20

When my aunt died I was just a little girl, only six years old. Before she died she had been living with my grandma for about a year because of her failing health. Really she was my grandmother's sister but everyone called her Auntie Eve.

About a week after the funeral my sister and I were at Grandma's house playing with Auntie Eve's costume jewellery that she kept in an old decorated box. We loved it all because it was so sparkly and gaudy. On this particular day I remember us asking Grandma where Auntie Eve had gone and her telling us that she was just gone and that we'd never see her again. Our mother told us that she was in heaven and that she was now with God. To the minds of small children all the grown-ups seemed to either be telling lies or not know the answers because they kept telling us different things.

At the time my sister was only four and didn't comprehend the seriousness of what had happened. I was really curious though, Auntie Eve was the first person I knew who had died and I was really curious as to what had happened to her. I remember lying on Auntie Eve's bed and asking aloud for her to tell me where she was so that I would know. I must have fallen asleep because the next thing I knew I my Auntie Eve was standing by my bed.

She looked very young and beautiful with long mahogany red hair. She held my hand and told me that she would be my companion and that she was waiting for me in the afterlife. Then it seemed as if a really cold wind was blowing through the room, I remember the curtains blowing even though the window was shut. When I woke up everything seemed back to normal, except that I was holding a book that I definitely didn't have when I went to sleep. The book was a French dictionary.

I took it downstairs and showed it to my grandmother. She told me that my Auntie Eve had loved languages and spoke fluent French. I told her about my dream and she looked so surprised. My Auntie Eve as I remember her had white hair and was old but my grandmother told me that when she was young she had long dark red hair. The only photographs I had seen of her were in black and white, I hadn't known that her hair was red. My grandmother told me that it was Eve coming to say goodbye and that I should keep the dictionary safely as it was her gift to me. That day I also went home with my Auntie Eve's jewellery.

I'm now at college, reading French and Spanish and still have the dictionary. I also kept the jewellery which I wear from time to time. It's now seen as cool and vintage, not how my mother and grandmother thought of it; 'Old junk!' they used to call it.

Karen, 20

My mum told me this story. When I was a baby, I became seriously ill with German measles. My dad had been killed in a car accident when my mum was pregnant with me so she was looking after me alone. Because I was so ill she was looking after me round the clock and was completely exhausted. One night at about 4am, she was sitting with me praying that I'd get better and, when she looked up, my dad was standing by my cot.

She told me that he put his hand on my forehead and said, 'She'll be alright'. He then disappeared but over the next twenty-four hours I began to make a spectacular recovery. It's nice to know that even though we've never met, he is looking after me.

Graham, 55

Some years ago I worked in farming and lived in a hundred-year-old cabin in the middle of nowhere. My nearest neighbour was four miles away and I didn't have a telephone. I have always enjoyed hunting and that was how I spent my weekends, walking in the woods with my shotgun.

One Sunday I accidentally shot myself in the leg after stumbling into a ditch. I wasn't really in any pain but I was losing a lot of blood. Out of nowhere I heard a voice telling me to get in the car and drive to a phone, I needed to get help fast. I got in the car and put my keys in the ignition. The voice told me to drive to the gas station and use the phone to call the emergency services. It was also reassuring me, 'Keep calm and you'll be alright. I will stay with you until help arrives.'

I drove to the gas station and asked to use the phone. When the boy who worked there saw me he came out from behind the counter and brought me some water and bound the wound with a cloth to reduce the blood flow.

We heard sirens in the distance and the voice said to me that it was leaving me but that I was about to lose consciousness. I could feel myself slipping into unconsciousness and when I woke up I was in hospital. The doctors told me that if I had lost consciousness earlier I would have died. What I didn't tell them is that the voice I heard was that of my best friend who had died four years previously when we were both twenty-three.

Ghostly Communications

Unexplained interaction with spirits

There are many so-called ghost stories telling us how, in certain places, the spirits of the dead can come through to this world and try to make contact, in some way, with those still living. These accounts are from those who have had experiences with the spirits of the dead where there is no clear-cut message or relationship, or at least where it is not so clear why the spirit chose to return to the material realm. Often the reason for these encounters with the dead remain unknown or the spirit needs psychic guidance to pass fully over into the afterlife.

Gillian, 19

My brother once tried to take some photographs of me using his cell phone camera. There was only myself, my brother and my parents in the house but that's not how it appeared on the photograph. There was only one of the photographs where I was the only person seen. In the rest, there were various bits of the face of a man, staring straight into the camera. We were both absolutely certain that he had not been in the room with us, but you couldn't deny that he was there in the images.

When we showed the pictures to my parents they didn't seem surprised. They told us that there had always been a bit of a strange atmosphere in the house, objects seemed to get moved or lost and they had always felt that there was a presence there besides them. My brother downloaded the images onto his computer and assembled a whole face of a man from the fragments on film. The features were clearly of a man aged between 30 and 40 wearing a white shirt and blue tie. He didn't exist in our household or neighbourhood. None of us had ever seen him before.

The next day we showed the image to some of our neighbours. Most of them said they had no idea who the man was. However, one guy who lived across the road told us that he had seen the man many times in our yard smoking. He said he could see him by his headlights in the dark but that whenever he turned his lights off he couldn't see him any more.

We now believe that the image was that of a ghost but

there have been others who have told us that because the image is digital, the existence of the face on the pictures could not easily be explained as supernatural because digital images can be manipulated so easily. However, we all know what we saw on those images, and what the guy over the road saw in our yard. We think he must be a man who lived in our house some time in the past.

He seems to be quite sociable, only making his presence felt when the house was inhabited and going outside to smoke to avoid polluting the air inside the house. My mother now occasionally puts a glass of whisky out for him in the evening. It never gets drunk overnight, but I think he probably appreciates the gesture.

Ben, 32

I was only twelve years old when this happened. At that time, we were living in a fairly large apartment complex in Florida. I remember that it was sunset and I was happily riding my blue bicycle around the streets near the complex. My mum had called for me twice already to come home. I was young and proud of my cycling skills and so I was happily ignoring her. None of the other children in the apartments owned a bike like mine and I rode it all the time, showing off.

As I was riding my bike along the sidewalk, I saw another little boy that I had never seen before. He certainly didn't live in our apartment complex. There were very few people walking by so he stood out. He was a little boy, about four feet tall, very dark skinned and fairly ordinary. He was looking directly at me, giving me a wide smile. His teeth were very white and he was wearing a bright yellow shirt.

At first I didn't think anything of it. He could have just moved to the area and be interested in bikes. Maybe he wanted to play with me and ride mine (No chance!).

I made a screechy one-wheeled right turn in front of him to demonstrate my skills. He remained smiling, there was absolutely no change in the way he was standing or the way he was looking at me. The following things struck me in the next few moments.

A man was walking along the sidewalk behind the boy in my direction but the boy didn't move an inch and seemed to be unaware of him. The next thing I saw terrified me. The man appeared to pass *straight through* the boy. He stayed standing and smiling at me as if nothing had happened. I stood there for maybe another two or three seconds then turned and pedalled towards home as fast as I could. As I turned into our road my heart nearly stopped.

The boy was standing in front of me just as before, same expression, same way of standing. I shut my eyes and pedalled furiously around him. I almost didn't open my eyes until I reached our building. We lived on the first floor and I had lost all my courage. I didn't want to go upstairs all alone. I shouted for my mum and she came down the stairs angry with me at first for not answering her calls and coming home. However, when she saw how shaken I was she asked me what the matter was and listened carefully as I told her. There was no way she believed me about strange boys smiling at me and decided it was a fanciful excuse for playing out late. She was kind to me though so I suppose she could at least tell that I was upset.

To this day I've tried to come up with many reasons as to why I saw this boy. I don't really believe in the supernatural but I can't think of any other reason for the visions I had that day. Perhaps he was playing tricks on me but how did he manage to move so fast? It's still an unexplained event from my childhood.

Colin, 34

I used to see a ghost in our back garden when I was a kid. I had to take the compost bucket down to the compost heap as one of my chores. I'd see this apparition, a faint image of a woman walking alongside me. She seemed to want to communicate something, but I couldn't hear what she was saying so she was frustrated.

I found it quite alarming. I told my mother I didn't want to go to the compost heap any more, especially in the winter when it was dark early. I told her about the ghost but of course she thought I was just making it up to try and get out of a chore.

In the end I stopped seeing her. I'm not sure if she

moved on to somewhere else or if I became less sensitive to these things as I got older.

Janice, 56

When I was a child we lived in a very old house that was quite secluded from the neighbours. It could only be reached by a long dirt track from the road a quarter of a mile away. During the winter the track would become very muddy and then become frozen over with ice.

I remember that every winter we had several visits from a neighbour who complained that we hadn't gritted the track road enough and told us that it was dangerous. She was a very old woman with long white hair and she was always eccentrically dressed in some kind of long wool dresses. I'd sometimes see her on our road shaking her head at me and pointing to the ice. My dad often went out with the grit late at night to help keep the road ice free and occasionally the county road crew would come by and do a more thorough job.

We never knew where the old woman lived but presumed it must be a little further down the track. She never told us her name and so became known as 'the winter lady' when we discussed her round the dinner table. We never did see her in spring or summer, only in the winter.

The winter I turned 18 we were in the local grocery store where mom was buying some coffee when she got talking to the man who owned the store. He was an elderly man whose family had lived in the area for several generations. Mom told him about our 'winter woman' and a strange look came over his face. He told mom that there was no elderly lady living down the track from us but said he remembered a story from his boyhood days about a woman who lived in what was now our house. He said that his grandfather had known her quite well because they had been at school together.

She was crazy about horses and always rode to school on hers. She never gave up riding even when she was an old lady. When she was 75 years old she had been riding her horse down the track just before Christmas when it slipped on the ice and fell. The horse was so badly injured that it had to be shot. She didn't die from her injuries, but was housebound after that and stayed that way until her death.

It turned out that our 'winter lady' was really someone who had died long ago. I guess it was her ghost communicating to us that we had to take better care of the track because it was dangerous. Or perhaps it was simply the regret she felt at losing her horse and her health that made her come back to us.

Sammy, 43

I have been sensing the presence of a spirit in the building where I work. I often stay late catching up on work as I have a fairly stressful job, so sometimes I will be the last person in the building.

On several occasions I have caught movement out of the corner of my eye as though someone was just entering or leaving the room. As soon as I look round whatever it is disappears, so I haven't seen what it looks like.

However, I also hear singing. It sounds like a woman's voice, humming a tune as she does something. My mother used to hum to herself as she did the ironing or the washing up and it is a similar kind of sound.

Finally I hear doors opening and closing from down the corridor.

I have done a small amount of research to see if someone died in this building or this particular location and thus far I can't find anything that would explain why there is a spirit there. I supposed I should find it scary but actually once I got used to it, I find it fairly ordinary. It doesn't seem like an angry or bad spirit. It seems more like a woman who is going about some everyday chores and singing herself a song as she does so.

Maybe one day I will see her. In the meantime I take the view that she isn't bothering me, so I shouldn't bother her.

Bob, 62

My grandmother told me a story about when she was a small girl, about 12 years old in Poland. At the time, she lived in a village with her extended family, in a house that had once been a farm. The family kept a herd of cows for their milk in a small barn that was the only outhouse on the property. The whole area was enclosed by an overgrown hedge.

She told me that one night as they were about to retire for the day, my grandmother and her sister had gone out through the kitchen into the small backyard that opened up to the barn. At that time there was a rumour about a tall, thin, old man covered in rags and with wounded legs that were supported by a stick. The story went that the man's legs were bandaged and his wounds crawled with maggots, he supposedly visited barns in order to get milk. The man also had a crippled wife, a bent-over old woman who would shake a bell attached to a stick she carried so as to warn people of the man's arrival. It was said that anyone who crossed him would face imminent death. After the man had got some milk for himself the rumour was that the cow who had given the milk could never be milked again. The milk would come out already sour forever afterwards.

My grandmother and her sisters had always thought the story as nothing more than a folk tale. On this particular night, my grandmother stood by the backyard door while her sister walked several yards to the washing line because she needed an item hung out to dry. While she stood there, my grandmother heard dogs barking frantically in the quiet night. It was then that she'd heard the tinkle of a bell coming from inside the barn.

She could also hear that the cows inside sounded

disturbed and restless. My grandmother considered what that sound was and was petrified. When her sister came back, she was stunned to see my grandmother standing still as a statue, eyes wide, trembling. Before she could ask what was going on, she heard the bell too. Grabbing my grandmother by the arm, she dragged her inside the house, locking the door. As they listened at the door my grandmother swears that she heard the voice of an old man telling them to, 'Leave this place, it's no good for you now.'

The next morning at breakfast the two girls told their parents who were a bit sceptical. However, when their mum went to milk the cows that morning it went sour within minutes. The same thing happened to every cow she milked. The family took the old man at his word and left the farm, eventually immigrating to the US.

Lew, 55

I have seen ghosts or spirits a few times in my life. There hasn't been anything especially dramatic about it. It's just something that seems to happen to me from time to time.

When I was thirteen I was looking out of my bedroom window when I saw a man walking along wearing a suit and a black hat. He didn't look like a ghost, he was just dressed in a slightly old-fashioned manner.

He walked right up our drive and I thought he was coming to visit. But then he just kept walking and went straight through the wall of the garage, as though it was water. That's how I knew he must be a spirit.

Another time I was staying at an old country house hotel in England. It was supposed to be haunted so it wasn't a huge surprise when I saw an apparition in the formal garden at dusk. It was a woman in a house-keeper's costume who came up to me and asked when the fire would be lit.

I asked her what she meant and she just looked confused and wandered off. I asked the owner about her and he said a few different people had seen her. She always asked questions about domestic arrangements but didn't seem to hear what anyone said in answer to her.

My wife doesn't see ghosts. I think she is a little bit jealous that they come to me. I don't know what I think really. It always makes me feel a little sad, to think of spirits who are stuck wandering the earth when they should have been able to move on to a better place.

Beryl, 56

When I was a child we lived in a large old house on the outskirts of New Orleans. I had one of the basement bedrooms which was OK, except that the basement didn't have air conditioning and the summers were very hot because the windows didn't open. I had a wooden rocking horse called Benny who I placed in the corner of the room so that I could see him from my bed.

Although there were few drafts in the room, Benny was perpetually in motion, rocking backwards and forwards and I loved to watch him. I remember one night I woke up to find a young man in the corner of my bedroom playing with the horse, moving it to and fro.

When I asked him who he was, he came to sit on the bed beside me and told me that his name was Jean and that we had been together in a different life and he was here to say hello.

I wasn't scared at all, in fact I felt very safe and comforted. I saw him many more times in my childhood. I would tell him about things at school and he would give me advice. It was clear that he cared about me a lot and I'm grateful to him for that.

Joe, 40

When I was a little boy, about eight or nine years old, I saw a man killed in a car accident. I was walking down Main Street when I heard the bang of a car and the screeching of brakes. All the people around me gasped and gathered in a crowd on the sidewalk to see what had happened.

When I looked out into the road I could see the man lying very still. He had blood coming from his head and was a strange purplish grey colour. Even though I was so young I knew he was dead. When the paramedics arrived they didn't even try to revive him, they just put him on a stretcher and covered him with a blanket.

Ever since then I have dreamed about it. I'm now 40 years old and still see him in my sleep. He's always saying things like, 'You saw it, tell someone'. I'm not sure what he means because there were a lot of people who saw the accident, not just me.

I'm quite scared of him actually. Whenever he is in my dreams I wake up feeling very anxious. I have no idea why this man has chosen to speak to me from beyond the grave or what I'm supposed to do with his messages.

Jill, 28

My ten-year-old son, Mark often tells me about his imaginary friend Toby. Mark insists that his friend isn't imaginary and tells me that he is someone who used to live in our house but died over 50 years ago.

Strangely, Mark told me that his friend used to go to a hill where the shopping mall is now and slide down the hill on sleighs in the snow. I went to our local library and looked at some old photographs of our town and I was amazed to see pictures of the hill and kids sliding in the snow on it. They must have levelled it to build the mall. Mark had also described an ironmonger's which was on the street where a beauty salon now stands.

He has told me so much about our town that I'm sure he couldn't possibly have known and if I check this information it is always exactly as Mark describes it to me. I think he really must be communicating with a guy who's been dead for 50 years!

Jenny, 30

We recently moved into a house in an area that used to be a military base. The army have moved on and the site is now a new housing development. From the day we moved into this house there was chaos. Things kept being moved from where they were put and pictures would fall off walls.

My husband told me that he was having dreams about an angry-looking soldier, wearing an officer's uniform, who shouted at him to get out of the house. I wonder if it was someone who had once lived there and who didn't understand that the house now belonged to us.

One morning I had had enough and stood in the middle of the kitchen and shouted at him and told him that this was our home now and he had to leave. I felt a warm breeze and suddenly the room smelled of flowers. I think he left because all the strange things have stopped happening.

Luke, 34

I had a series of vivid dreams recently. A young woman dressed in peasant's clothing kept knocking on my door and then asking me to come and help her family.

Most times I woke up before the dream got any further. But one time I managed to get my coat on. She led me outside and I realised that it was the town I live in now, but a long time in the past.

She took me to a wooden house which no longer exists. A family of three adults and four children were sat outside with all their possessions in a pile. It looked as though they were being evicted. The young woman once again asked me to help. I tried to ask her how I could help, but then I woke up again.

It might just be a dream, but the vision I had of our town in the past was extremely convincing. I do wonder if it is some kind of spiritual communication, perhaps resulting from a traumatic moment in this young woman's life.

Alison, 22

My sister Hannah said that one night she woke up to find the whole room shaking violently. She could hear people, a man and a woman, arguing in the hallway outside the bedroom. She got up and went to see if her son's computer was switched on and playing something from YouTube but it wasn't. Once again she went back to bed, but no sooner had she got back into bed than she heard the voices again. They were arguing about who had left the door open.

Hannah got up but she still couldn't see anyone. She

went downstairs and looked in all the rooms but the TV wasn't on and she could see nobody. Just before she climbed the stairs again she glanced at the front door. It was ajar. She swears that she closed and locked the door before going up to bed.

She was quite frightened that she must have an intruder but she checked everywhere and no one was in the house except her and her son. Also, nothing was missing. She re-locked the door and went back to bed.

She now thinks that the voices were ghosts but she isn't sure if they were re-enacting an old argument or perhaps simply warning her that the house wasn't secure.

Meg, 37

Some years ago I was alone in our house watching TV. My husband is a firefighter and he was on a late shift. I suddenly heard three loud knocks on the back door. I turned down the TV and listened again. This time I heard the knocks again but they were slower than the first time. I had thought that it could be the wind but because of the change of speed of them I decided to have a look to see what it was. I went into the kitchen but I couldn't see anything.

When my husband came home from work I told him about it and he went out into the yard to see if it could have been a burglar or a wild animal. He came in clutching a white handkerchief with a blue border. It didn't belong to either me or my husband.

We never found out who the handkerchief belongs to. The whole thing gave me a rather strange feeling. And in the weeks following that I often had dreams about a man knocking at the back door. He was middle-aged and wearing a smart suit. It seemed like he lived in the house and just wanted someone to let him in.

It hasn't happened for a while but it makes me nervous if I hear any knocking in the house now, even if it just the chidren playing.

Jim, 31

In elementary school I always used to see children in our classroom who were not in our class. Some of these children were my friends but there was one problem. None of the other kids could see them. One day I was sitting in the library corner talking to one of the invisible children when the teacher asked me who I was talking to. When I told her, she called me a naughty boy and a liar. I told the boy to go away and I never saw him again.

Even though I am now thirty-one, I still see children. As far as I can understand, they are the spirits of dead children. I've just moved house and there is a little girl in my wardrobe who sniffles most of the night. I'm sure she threw a coat hanger at me late one night. It clanged on the bed then fell on the floor. I wish I could get rid of these children but I can't.

Charlie, 26

When I was thirteen we moved house and for some reason I always felt that there was something strange about the atmosphere in it. About two years later I was sitting watching TV in the school holidays when my dog Vampy began barking at the window as if there was an intruder out there.

I pulled him back and tried to calm him down but his hackles were raised and he went straight back to the window and carried on barking. I went over to the window to see what the problem was and at first I couldn't see anything but then I noticed a little girl wearing a blue dress sitting on the ground at the very back of the lawn where there was some shrubbery. She appeared to be crying and when she looked up at me she beckoned for me to come outside as if she wanted me to help her.

I went into the kitchen and out of the back door but when I got into the garden there was no one there. I went to the back of the lawn and looked amongst the bushes there but I couldn't see anything. The undergrowth in that bit of the garden at the time was very thick, it was virtually impossible to step into the shrubs. In fact, my dad had arranged for someone to come and thin them out in about two weeks time. I thought that the girl must have just run off and went back inside to carry on watching TV.

A couple of weeks later two workmen came round to clear that section of the garden of some of the older denser bushes. After they had been working for about three hours, one of the men found a bit of blue fabric that looked as if it was part of a bit of clothing. However, when they began to pull it up they found the bones of a small human hand. They immediately called the police who cordoned off the area.

They found the partial remains of a child's skeleton. No one ever managed to identify her, it's impossible to be sure how long she had been there. The girl I had seen was wearing a blue dress. I've wondered ever since whether or not this girl was trying to tell me where her body was buried so that she could be given a proper burial and blessing.

Lesley, 42

In 1995 I bought an old house built sometime in the 1880s. It was a nice, big, comfortable house and I was delighted to move in. However, not long afterwards I began to hear knocking on the door, whenever I went to check there was no one there.

Another time I was sitting in the kitchen reading the newspaper when the blinds at the window began swaying. When I went over to them they stopped completely, and when I tried to move them they didn't seem able to sway.

Electrical things such as the radio and microwave began switching themselves on even though I knew that I had switched them off. One day I could hear a tap running upstairs and when I went up to investigate it looked as if someone was trying to run a bath. It wasn't me and I was in the house alone. The whole bathroom was steamed up by the hot water and as I looked around I saw what looked like a hand print on the bathroom mirror. It couldn't have been mine because it was too small and it couldn't have been my sons because he was at school.

A couple of weeks later it was my son's birthday and we had a party. As the boys sang happy birthday I took some pictures of them. When we got the film developed there seemed to be a strange girl in one of them. Her image wasn't solid like the other children but she was definitely there. I decided to investigate the history of my house.

I went to the local library and began looking into the archives for any information I could get. I told the librarian what information I was looking for and she was very helpful. She found me an obituary of a woman called Sarah who had died at the age of 19 in the house in 1922.

I went back home and said 'Hello Sarah,' loudly. There was instantly a sweet smell and the whole house felt lighter.

The strange thing is that since that day there have been no more weird happenings in the house. I think that Sarah just wanted me to know that she was still around. Now I know her name she's content to leave us alone.

Gita, 26

I was engaged to be married when I was nineteen. I remember waking up to find a woman standing by my bed. She looked at me for a few seconds and then said, 'Think about it, no good will come of it.' At first I didn't understand. I loved my fiancé very much and the wedding had been meticulously planned, the invitations sent out and all the details had been sorted out.

Four months later I got married and from the first day of our honeymoon my husband's attitude towards me changed. He became moody and possessive. One night at our hotel in the Maldives he slapped me in the face because I had smiled to one of the waiters in the restaurant. Things got worse when we got home. He refused to spend any money eating out or buying nice food at the grocery store. He also wouldn't allow me to go out to work so I had no income.

Every night when he got home from work he inspected every inch of our house and if he found a bit of dust or dirty mark he would get angry and violent. I left him after four months. Now I know why the spirit in my room was warning me not to get married.

Colleen, 45

I used to see the ghost of my Aunt Rachel. She had died in her fifties. I used to see her walking through our garden and two times I saw her in our kitchen looking out of the window.

One time I woke up and she was standing next to the bed. She seemed to be trying to say something to me.

I find it quite puzzling. She is not someone I was close to in my life. My Uncle Frank and my father argued about money when I was a kid and they rarely saw each other. I probably only saw her at family occasions and they were always a bit awkward as one half of the family wasn't speaking to the other half. I don't remember her being especially interested in me back then.

Perhaps she feels regretful about the way things went wrong in our family. Life really is too short to let petty feuds spoil family relationships. I suppose you always think that there is plenty of time, but when someone dies you realise that isn't always true. My Uncle Frank and my father never did make up – Frank died last year and my dad didn't even go to the funeral.

Veronica, 36

I have the spirit of a little boy in my house. He often appears at night and asks me to help him cross over to the other side. Just before I see him I get a headache and feel out of breath. He whispers in my ear when I'm sitting watching TV.

One time he told me that his name is Richard and he died of tuberculosis in 1858 when he was seven years old.

I have told him to go but he says he doesn't want to. I'm about to contact a medium to try and get him to cross over into the light.

I have been able to connect with spirits since I was around ten years old. The house I grew up in had two spirits in it. One was an eight-year-old girl who said her name was Emma and used to come and play with me sometimes when I was alone in my bedroom. The other spirit was an old man who was very bad-tempered and used to make the shelves rattle when I was trying to sleep. I was the only person who could see and hear these spirits and my parents never believed me.

Andrea, 18

My best friend thinks that her house is haunted and one night we decided to try to communicate with whoever the spirit was. It was just me and my friend Adele. We lit candles and sat on the floor. I asked the spirit to come forward and at exactly that moment I felt someone push me in the back.

After that I don't remember anything until Adele was shaking me and shouting at me. Apparently, I'd begun talking in a strange voice and told her that my name was Beatrice and I'd lived in the house a long time ago. Beatrice had died of pneumonia when she was thirty-two years old. Her favourite room was Adele's bedroom because that used to be her room when she was a child. She said that she didn't mean anyone any harm.

It was me saying all those things according to Adele and I was lying on the floor with my eyes shut. To me it felt as if I'd passed out, I certainly must have lost consciousness for a while. Adele is happier because we talked to the spirit and it's not malevolent.

Beatrice, 19

My father used to be a miner and when I was around fifteen years old we lived in a small mining community in Wales. I was dating my first boyfriend, Nick, and one summer night I went over to his house when he had to babysit for his little brother. I took along some homework and we sat at the kitchen table answering a biology question paper. Sean, my boyfriend's little brother asked if he could play outside and we agreed and told him not to stray beyond the row of houses we were in.

It was a lovely summer evening but I started to feel cold and asked Nick to lend me a jumper. He told me to go up and get one and I went upstairs but as I climbed the stairs I began to feel colder and colder. I grabbed a jumper and put it on before going downstairs. Half way down the stairs the lights in the bathroom began to flick on and off. I told Nick and he came upstairs with me to try to find out what was going on.

While we were standing on the landing we heard footsteps on the kitchen floor below. It was an old cottage had had the original stone floors that had been put in when it was built. We could distinctly hear footsteps walking around the kitchen. Thinking it must be Sean we went back downstairs. However, when we got downstairs the kitchen was empty.

We then heard footsteps upstairs and Nick ran up shouting at Sean to stop playing tricks because we had to do our homework but, once again, there was no one up there. He searched every room upstairs and then came back down asking me if I'd seen Sean; I hadn't. Suddenly we heard a child's giggling and the footsteps upstairs started again. This time the hall lights began to flick on and off. I ran into the street and I could see Sean playing with his friends on the street corner. I told Nick that it couldn't be Sean and we sat at the table wondering what could be going on. Eventually, I felt so spooked that I wanted to go home. Nick asked me to at least stay until his parents got back. We were both quite scared so we went out into the back garden and sat at the table there.

When Nick's mum and dad came home we told them about what had happened. They said that they too had had some weird experiences in the house and told us that they had done a bit of research on the house's history but hadn't been able to find out what had happened there in the past.

Nick's parents eventually asked a priest to come in and bless the house. From then on Nick said they heard a few childish giggles now and then, but the house was much calmer and the footsteps stopped.

Carrie, 53

My daughter Susie is now twenty-eight, but when she was thirteen something strange happened. She had been visiting friends with her dad and they stayed quite late, not driving home until nearly midnight.

The roads around where we lived were often deserted at that time of night so they were surprised to see a woman walking down the road alone in front of their car. She was wearing a long summer dress even though it was late September and starting to become much cooler at night time and in her arms she was carrying a small bundle wrapped in cloth.

As the car got closer to her she turned around and stared at Susie and her dad, then held out her arms as if offering them something. They could see that the parcel she was carrying was a baby in a blanket. Then as the car braked to avoid hitting her she simply disappeared. When they looked out of both the front and back windows of the car she had gone.

Both Susie and her dad told people about the incident and were eventually told a story about a homeless woman who had given birth in the fields and had been killed by a speeding car as she tried to make her way to hospital. Apparently, many drivers have seen her try to get a lift to hospital. Maybe she didn't know that she'd died and has been walking the road to get to hospital ever since her accident.

Animal Spirits

Being helped and comforted by
much loved deceased pets

As humans, we become very attached to our animals and pets, often nearly as much as we do to the human members of our families. When alive, these creatures will sit with us when we need comfort and show gratitude when we comfort them.

Some of the accounts in this section show us that the spirits of these special animals can also communicate with us from beyond the grave. They enjoyed being with us just as much as we loved being with them. Meanwhile, others show us that animals can sometimes be more sensitive to the world of spirits than people.

Jack, 50

When I was a little boy we had a dog called Bingo. He lived in a big kennel under a large tree in the yard and it was my job to give him food and water and take him for walks. He was my best friend and I was always sure that there was something different about him. Bingo was a very happy dog. He acted like he was still a puppy his whole life, he was always playful, barking and jumping around.

One day when I went outside to be with him he behaved differently from how he usually did. He put his head in my lap and looked up at me with what I can only describe as an expression of such love and devotion that I began to be worried that he was sick. About six weeks later we found him dead in the yard. Apparently he had an inoperable tumour that we hadn't known about.

Later that night I woke up in my bedroom to the unmistakeable sound of barking from the yard. I grabbed my boots and ran outside in my pyjamas. I swear that Bingo was there in the yard, leaping about just as usual. I sat under the tree and he came over to me and rested his head on my lap just as he had before. I put my head on the top of his head and told him how much I loved him.

The next morning my parents found me alone, asleep in my pyjamas under the tree. I told them about Bingo but they said I must have been dreaming. I'm 50 years old now but I'm still sure that my dog came back to me that night because he wanted to say goodbye.

Cleo, 64

I think that my cat must be able to see spirits. She often looks up and miaows as though she is looking at someone, though I can't see anyone there. I also see her rubbing against someone's legs. It is exactly the same motions she makes when she rubs my legs, but there is no one there. To start with I found this habit quite disconcerting but now I have got used to it.

At least it seems like whoever it is she usually sees is a nice spirit. The cat is always pleased to see him or her and she purrs a lot when the spirit is there.

Only once did she react badly to something. She suddenly leapt up from where she was sleeping and started hissing or spitting at something that she could see but I couldn't. It made the hairs on the back of my neck stand up when I saw that.

At the time I felt quite alarmed, as though she had seen an evil spirit. But it didn't happen again and, the more I think about it, the more I think maybe she just saw the ghost of another cat. She is very territorial and would be furious if another cat came into her house!

Toby, 58

Sometimes at night, my wife Emma is convinced that she sees the spirit of our dog Jack asleep by the side of our bed. She loved that dog so much and now believes that he still comes back to visit her.

I have read that it is when the human and animal bond is close that the spirits of animals can come back to visit us. That dog was always following her around when he was alive so it's perhaps no surprise that he comes back to see her now and again.

Karen, 32

I am twenty-five years old and a practising Wiccan. I have been involved with Wicca since I was fourteen. I have always had a strong belief in the afterworld and believe that we can communicate with dead spirits.

In the Wicca religion we believe in having a familiar, but unfortunately I lost mine just after the Summer Solstice. Simsi was my best friend, a Burmese cat who used to sleep on my lap or next to me in bed and we used to talk to each other all the time.

Two days before Christmas he got hit by a car in front of my house in the early hours of the morning. I was so full of grief when I found him that I just stood shrieking in the middle of the road. I probably woke up the whole street.

When I finally could think straight, I made Simsi a coffin in a box I lined with one of my shirts that he used to like to sleep on and buried him in the garden.

I told his spirit that he could come and visit me

whenever he wanted. As I lay in bed that night crying for my Simsi, I suddenly felt a weight lie down beside me just as Simsi had done.

The next feeling was of a paw across my chest in the way that Simsi would do when I was upset. He would always come to me and pat my face and stretch out across me as if he was giving me a hug.

Suddenly the room felt full of warmth and I knew Simsi was back. I have now felt his loving energy on many occasions. I have bought a new kitten that I'm training to become my familiar but every so often he runs away skittishly as if being chased. When that happens I say 'Simsi, you stop it', and the kitten comes back.

Dan, 24

My brother John passed away about five years ago and communicates with me through animals. He died on Christmas Day 2005. He began to contact me the day after he died.

At that time he would leave sprigs of holly whenever he had been around me and when I found them I would know that they were from him. Whenever I was in need of some spiritual comfort I would find a sprig of holly.

He then began contacting me through animals. I was walking my daughter to school one day when a blackbird swooped down in front of me then landed on the branch of a tree just above my head.

The bird seemed to eye me with amusement and when I looked down there was a sprig of holly at my feet. When I picked it up the bird began to sing and then flew off. I just know that it was something to do with my brother. I see the blackbird several times a week and there is often a sprig of holly somewhere when I see the bird.

He has also come to me as a honey bee. He loved honey when he was alive and at one point even considered bee keeping. If I'm driving I often see a honey bee hovering around the windscreen and get that familiar excitable feeling when I know that my brother is contacting me again.

The Christmas after he died the whole family got together for Christmas dinner and looking out onto the lawn I saw a white hare sitting upright and still on the lawn. John had a thing about hares, about how special and unique they were.

The thing that convinced me that the hare was a message from my brother was something that happened the next day, Boxing Day.

I had arranged to visit Mel who had been John's girlfriend when he died. As soon as I got through the door she told me about the white hare she had seen in her garden on Christmas Day.

We live in a village, not the country and seeing one hare is a very rare thing especially in winter but to see two is very unlikely. I think my brother wanted to wish everyone Merry Christmas.

Moira, 64

In the last few years of my mother's life she was fairly weak, having broken a hip in a fall. Most days I would drive round to her house and pick her up after I dropped the kids at school. Then she would come back with me and sit on the sofa watching telly and chatting to me as I did the housework.

I'd sit with her for a while in the afternoon, then she was happy to be able to spend time with her grand-children when they came home from school.

She'd stay through the evening meal and then my husband would run her home in the car. It was nice to have her around – it was probably the most time I'd spent with her since I was a kid and she told me a lot of funny stories about people she had known when she was younger. She seemed very dignified and sensible in old age, but she was a bit of a tearaway when she was younger and some of her stories were hilarious and even quite rude.

Often in the morning, while I was doing the ironing, our Jack Russell dog would jump up and sit next to her. That was the only time he was allowed on the sofa. I thought it was nice for her to have him keeping her company.

She would be sitting at the left hand end of the sofa. He would jump up, turn around three times and then flop down next to her, in the exact middle of the sofa. Then he would look up at her and wag his tail while she talked to him.

She passed away earlier this year, from pneumonia, which some people call the 'old people's friend'. I don't think she suffered too much and she had done well to make it to eighty-eight years old.

But of course I miss her, and there isn't a day goes by when I don't think of something I have to remember to tell her, or think of a funny story I could remind her of. Then I have to pull myself up as I remember that she is no longer with us.

However, sometimes I wonder how far she has really gone. The dog still isn't allowed on the sofa. But since her death, he sometimes jumps up in exactly the same way in the mornings.

He turns around three times and then flops down in exactly the place he used to sit next to her. Then he sits there looking up at the space where she used to sit, wagging his little tail.

I can't help but wonder if he is sensing her presence when he does this. It doesn't happen every day, but it is quite often and when he looks up like that I don't have the heart to chase him off on to the floor.

I have taken to chatting to my mum when he sits there looking up at her like that. I can't be sure whether she is really there or not, but if she is I like to think she can hear the things I tell her.

Maybe the dog is more sensitive to her presence than a person would be and can tell when her spirit comes to see me.

Louise, 20

When I was a little girl my granddad bought me a horse that I called Lightning. I loved that horse; he was all white with a very long mane and tail. I only fell off him once and he stood by making a lot of noise until someone heard and came to see what was happening. I had banged my head and was woozy with concussion. We were very close and I knew that he loved me as much as I loved him. Sadly he died when I was ten years old and I was so upset I cried for weeks.

One night in the year after he had died I woke up and could hear a horse making a lot of noise outside. I looked out of my bedroom window towards the fields and to my astonishment I thought I saw Lightning out in the garden whinnying. I shouted out to him, and this woke the whole family up. When dad went downstairs to see what was going on he found smoke drifting up the stairs. The living room was on fire because he hadn't put his cigarette out properly, and the fire was about to spread into the hallway at the bottom of the stairs.

I think that Lightning is still looking after me. He came back from the dead to save me and my family.

George, 49

My sister Amy was diagnosed with lung cancer in 2001. She had chemotherapy for six months but it didn't work and by January 2002, she knew her illness was terminal.

The whole family visited her all the time, especially when she was moved to the hospice, to make sure she was never on her own. I remember one visit I made to her bedside with my other sister Lilia. Amy was looking out of the window at the garden when a large butterfly came into view. We all watched it for a while. It was really unusual, quite large and a purple or violet colour. It was really beautiful. Amy said that if there was such a thing as reincarnation, she wanted to come back as a butterfly like that one. She died in July 2002.

The night before her funeral, I had a dream where I was following a butterfly just like the one we had seen outside the window of the hospice. I woke up remembering the conversation Amy, Lilia and I had had and wondered if it was some kind of message from Amy or if her death was playing tricks on my mind by making my unconscious remembering a conversation with my dead sister.

However, at the funeral, a large violet butterfly flew around the flowers left at the graveside by the mourners and I began to be sure that it was Amy saying goodbye to everyone and thanking them for coming to say goodbye to her.

Another time I was driving home from work when a purple butterfly landed on my windscreen. I couldn't see properly for it and pulled to the side of the road to chase it away. I got out of the car and wafted at the butterfly. As I did so a truck on the road skidded sideways and shed its load of construction equipment across the highway. If I hadn't have stopped the car I could have been hit and badly injured, quite possibly even killed.

I told this story to my wife who believes that the butterfly is Amy dropping by to say hello. I certainly see a lot more of those purple butterflies than I used to before Amy died.

Rosa, 26

A few years ago, I used to have a cat called Molly. At the time I lived in a basement apartment that was cheap and not very nice. Back then, it was all I could afford.

In my bedroom was a wooden rocking chair that had been in the apartment since I moved in. I often left my clothes on it at night because my cat wouldn't go near the chair so the clothes wouldn't get cat hairs on them.

One night I was woken by a loud crash. I put the lamp on and looked around the room. The chair was rocking back and forth. I wondered if the cat had been on it and jumped off but I couldn't see her anywhere. I wondered about earthquakes. About two minutes later the cat poked her head round the door, came in took one look at the chair and began growling. Her tail fluffed out as if he were angry or frightened.

A few months later my bedside table fell over with a loud crash in the middle of the night. This time the cat was sleeping on my bed and also woke up, growling as before. I tried telling myself that it must have been an earth tremor, but nothing else was out of place. Suddenly the cat jumped off the bed and walked to the chair. As he turned to me he had a funny expression on his face and he continued to growl.

The next day I spoke to one of my upstairs neighbours who told me that an old man had died in my apartment six months earlier. Apparently he was very antisocial, never had visitors and usually didn't say as much as hello to anyone. I became sure that he was still in my apartment and didn't want to share it with anyone. I moved out two weeks later and had no further trouble in the night.

Lena, 26

When I was a little girl I lived with my grandparents and so I was very close to them. My grandfather died first, about three years before my grandmother, and I know she missed him in her later years.

The night before my grandmother died I went to visit her in hospital. She held my hand and said, 'You know how much I love you, I'll never be far away, look out for me.' She passed away that night.

At the funeral there was a robin in the tree outside the chapel and I thought it meant something because I knew that it was my grandmother's favourite bird. When we went back to my house for the wake, I looked out into the garden and again there was a robin. For the next week I kept seeing robins everywhere I went, always just one. It was my grandmother telling me that she was alright.

Even now I'll get a strange feeling as if someone has tapped my shoulder and I'll turn around and there won't be anyone there but there'll be a robin watching me.

Ouija Boards and Evil Spirits

Tales of caution when contacting the spirit world

There are many tales which suggest we should exercise great caution when contacting the spirit world. For those with a psychic ability, the spirits will come to them through meditation or channelling through appropriate equipment. If other spirits want to send us a personal message, they will do so.

However, if the inexperienced open the division between the afterlife and our life, the consequences can be frightening. There seem to be many evil or troubled entities and spirits who will use any opportunity to create havoc in our world. The stories in this section cover a variety of experiences and a number of them provide excellent illustrations of what that can go wrong when people try to force spirits to communicate with us.

It seems worthwhile including a few of these less pleasant stories as a warning that communication with the dead is not something to be taken lightly.

Bess, 18

My mum died at a very young age, I was so devastated that I couldn't accept it. I wanted to talk to her again, to make sure that she was alright and happy. One day, I was hanging out with my friends and one of them suggested trying to contact the dead. I agreed to it because all I could think of was trying to talk to my mum again. We decided to do it on the night of Halloween. One of my friends' parents were going out for the evening, so we decided to go to her house where we would have the place to ourselves.

There were six of us and we were both excited and nervous as we prepared for the big night. At around 7pm, we all sat in a circle, laughing and giggling, thinking this may be kind of stupid and not wanting to make fools of ourselves. We all argued over who would be the one to speak and it was eventually agreed that I would do it because I wanted to try to contact my mum. We all joined hands and lit a candle in the centre of the circle, which was the only light in the room. I asked the spirit world to come to us.

Suddenly, one of the girls shouted out that she felt we were being contacted by an evil spirit. She seemed really frightened. I had started by asking my mum to come and talk to us. I don't know whether I fell asleep or went into a deep trance, but suddenly I felt like I wasn't in the room with my friends. I was very scared and my body was trembling but I couldn't move. I felt like something was holding me down. I couldn't open my eyes or speak.

Then I felt a hard slap on my shoulder and I fell over. I was then back in the room with the others. I looked around and everyone was sitting there with utter disbelieve on their faces. My friends told me that I had risen up slightly from the floor, almost levitating, and then swayed from side to side. I had been speaking with a different voice, more like a man's voice, threatening everyone.

We were all pretty frightened. It seemed that in opening the door to the spirit world and asking my mum to come to me we had unwittingly brought in an evil spirit. We ran out of the house that night and we never did anything like that again.

Stacy, 16

My name is Stacy. I have lived many lives before this one. I'm only 16 years old but I can talk to any spirit because I'm partly from the spirit world. Since I was little I've been able to see lots of things. Sometimes I see scary things like demons. It's cool and nerve-wracking at the same time, but I also taught myself to not be afraid of them. Some are nice and some are mean. I also learned to talk with them and go to the shadow realm. I don't know if you have heard of it. To go in you must be ready for anything. Anyhow I can't tell you exactly what they look like, because they don't all look the same.

Kay, 27

When I was in college I went with a friend, Billy to Jake's, her boyfriend's apartment for some food and drinks. As the evening wore on someone suggested that we play the Ouija board. I was a bit frightened by the thought of it but I'd had a couple of beers and eventually everyone persuaded me to join in. By some fluke I was wearing my father's shirt. He had died almost exactly six months earlier. I really missed him and often wore his clothes to feel closer to him. We lit some candles and set the Ouija board up on the floor. It suddenly felt as if I couldn't breathe, as if there wasn't enough oxygen in the room.

The others asked who the Ouija wanted to speak to and it began to spell out part of my childhood nickname, Peanut. None of the others could possibly have known that this was my nickname. They asked who was speaking and it spelled out the first few letters of my father's name.

I wanted to stop right there but the others were getting

excited about communicating with the dead. The planchette carried on moving and then spelled out 'Joke', and the room became freezing cold.

We all sensed that we were dealing with a malevolent spirit. It wasn't my father but another spirit here to play with us. Suddenly one of the candles blew out and everyone screamed. I couldn't find the door of the room to get out and the others didn't seem to be able to take their fingers off the planchette.

One of Jake's roommates came home and heard us screaming. He opened the door and it was as if something swept out of the room and everything became calm. None of us ever spoke about it again.

Chris, 20

I received a message from my grandfather via a medium who used a Ouija board. He died when I was just six years old so I really wasn't expecting it. He told me that he was pleased with my exam results which surprised me because I hadn't even got the results at that point. (I did actually get straight A's for every subject).

He also told me not to waste time with Sophie, (my then girlfriend) because I would soon meet someone who was better for me. I had been having lots of arguments with Sophie about going to college. We ended the relationship that weekend and I did meet a girl at college who I'm now very happily married to. Many people seem to have had very bad experiences with Ouija boards but I have to say that mine was very positive.

Jasmine, 20

When we were teenagers two of my friends and I got interested in Ouija boards and made one ourselves to have a try at playing it. During our first few tries, two of us would put our fingers on the spinner and the other would write everything down with a pad and pen. At first we enjoyed it, we seemed to contact spirits who were perhaps telling us about their lives and it was quite interesting. Then a couple of weeks after we had started playing with it, things began to get weird and we started to become frightened.

One spirit came through and he wasn't nice like the other spirits. The thing was, we couldn't get rid of him. He said a lot of things to scare us. One night he just spelled the words 'Die alone.' Then he said, 'Not a toy', which we took to mean the Ouija board and we stopped playing it because it freaked us out so much.

The following year one of my friends' sisters died in a car accident. She was her big sister and they were very close. A couple of months after the funeral my friend came to see me to ask if we could try the Ouija board to get in touch with her sister. I was a bit hesitant but eventually agreed to give it a go. Nothing happened so we gave up.

A month later my other friend who had played with the Ouija board with me lost her father in an industrial accident. I immediately put the thing in the bin. I will never ever use one again.

Isla, 33

I used to live in a house where there was an evil spirit. My husband thought I was losing my mind. I had a young child at the time and had been through a period of depression after the birth. But I wasn't imagining the spirit. It used to break things and come into my dreams and threaten me. It kept asking me to 'let it out'. I didn't know what that meant but it seemed like a truly bad idea.

In the end I got a priest round without telling my husband. He told me that he didn't believe in exorcism but nonetheless he agreed to come round and bless the house. He brought some holy water and a bible and sat with me in the front room saying a prayer and putting his blessing on the house.

Thankfully it seemed to work. I have not felt that presence since the priest's visit.

Jonny, 23

I once watched my girlfriend play the Ouija board with some of her friends at a party. I watched the plastic pointer move and the girls would giggle and I presumed that someone was moving it on purpose. I didn't believe that it would move on its own. They were trying to contact the man who built the house. My girlfriend lived in a house built in the early nineteenth century and always said that it was full of ghosts.

They asked for the spirits to come forward and a man's name was spelled out. At the time I thought that they were making it up. The pointer spelled out a name and then went on to indicate the number 1859. It then spelled out the word, 'Hang'. It was all very specific information and I made a note of the name, if only to prove to my girlfriend that I knew that they were playing a practical joke on me.

About a week later I was in town and decided to go to the library to see if the Ouija board was as in touch with the spirits of the departed as so many people claim it to be.

I looked up the archives for our local paper for the year 1859 and to my amazement a man of that exact name had been murdered at my girlfriend's address in 1859. His killer, one of the neighbours, was convicted and hanged for his crime the following year. I don't see how any of the girls could have known that.

Kate, 40

I often feel evil spirits around me in places where something bad has happened in the past. I don't know why, but I seem to be able to sense their presence.

I take the firm view that I do not want to listen to them or hear what they have to say. I think that if you open yourself up to evil then you are putting yourself in danger.

Daphne, 22

When we were teenagers, my best friend Sally and I used to play witchcraft with an old pendulum that had belonged to her grandmother. We had heard a story that a murder had been committed in the house in the 1950s, in an attic bedroom.

One night when I was sleeping over at her house we decided to try to contact the spirit of the supposed murder victim. At midnight we turned out all the lamps and lit a candle. At first we were just trying to scare each other swinging the pendulum back and forth but then Sally suddenly held it still and asked if there were any spirits who wanted to talk to us.

The pendulum began swinging in a circle very forcefully. We then asked if the spirit had lived in the house before, telling the pendulum to swing clockwise for yes and anti-clockwise for no. The pendulum spun in a clockwise direction. Sally cut out the letters of the alphabet and we put them in a row then asked the spirit what their name was.

The pendulum pointed to the letters BILL. When we asked if he died in the house it span clockwise. Then the pendulum started to go a bit haywire and swung around violently. Sally kept asking what it wanted and the pendulum spelled out ANGRY. Suddenly there was a strong blast of cold air. At the same time we heard a loud bang as if the door had been slammed. We were both very frightened and ran to the light switch to turn the light back on.

All our screaming and banging woke Sally's mum up and she came to see what the matter was. When we told her she was pretty disappointed in us. She told us that we'd been meddling with the supernatural and made us pray for the spirit to rest in peace.

I have always wondered what those words meant but I guess if I learned one thing it is that it is not a good idea to try and contact the dead.

Valerie, 19

I lived in college dorms last year and about a month ago I woke up suddenly in the night. There was a sound like wind blowing into my ear and a spiteful female voice said, 'No waiting'. I then felt like something very heavy was pressing on my chest. I couldn't get to sleep for the rest of the night.

The next night I was woken again by the same voice telling me to go away. It said 'I don't want you here'. I was so scared that I told some of friends about it the next day and two others had had a similar experience. We asked around and several people had heard a voice whisper jealous, spiteful things to them.

We had no idea why these things had happened. Some of the girls wanted to organise an exorcism but I found the whole idea scary. While other girls just didn't take it seriously. In the end I moved out of the dorms and went to stay in my friend's apartment instead. I don't know whose voice it was and I don't want to know.

Kathleen, 20

A bunch of friends and I decided to have a séance at my cousin's twenty-first birthday party. We went up to the guest room where we were all supposed to be staying that night and set everything up.

We sat in a circle with four candles lit in the centre and we all held hands. One of my friends, Alice, had done a séance before and she asked out loud if there were any spirits who wanted to talk to us. Nothing happened except us giggling for a while but suddenly, another of my friends, Jeanie started to cry. We asked her what the matter was but all she could say was, 'I'm only little, I'm only little'. It was weird because it wasn't her voice, she sounded like someone much, much younger. Then she began pleading 'No, no'.

In her strange voice, Jeanie told us that her name was Annabel and she was nine years old. She told us that she had been locked in the closet then a man had opened the door and strangled her. Jeanie began screaming and ran out of the room. I followed her downstairs where she was back to herself but very frightened. She said she had been able to feel hands on her throat. The rest of our group came running downstairs as well.

That night none of us could sleep in that room. We could all feel a malicious presence. Then Alice said that we'd forgotten to close the circle and we had to close it. We all reluctantly got up and sat in the circle again, holding hands. Alice told all spirits to leave, that we were closing off the division between our world and theirs.

Alice told us all to keep on holding hands whatever happened. There were two very loud bangs and a pile of books fell off the dresser. After that things felt a bit calmer and we managed to go back to bed but we kept the lamp on all night.

Heather, 17

I have often seen a man accompanying me when I'm awake. Whenever I see him I'm always frightened. I have no idea who he is but I can sense that his presence is malevolent. Once, when I was at school, I saw him in our sitting room on a day when I was off sick with chicken pox.

Very late at night I saw lots of dead people materialise in the room. Some of them were decomposing in front of me with rotting flesh and missing eyeballs. I ran out of the room but I could hear them coming after me. They were shouting 'kill her, kill her'. This went on most of the night no matter where I ran to. The next day I told my parents but they didn't believe me.

I also sometimes see a dead child who points at me and tells me to come with her. She is often standing by the bed with her face close up to mine and a look of hatred on her face. Sometimes she rattles my bed to wake me up. I put a spell on my bedroom door to keep her and the other dead people out but sometimes they still get through.

I know they're here even if I can't see them because my cat won't get on the bed. My cat sometimes sits facing the bedroom door as if he can hear something outside it. He also gets that look on his face that cats get when they're staring at something waiting for a fight.

My last encounter with dead people was a few days ago. I woke up to hear lots of noises as if someone was rushing through the house in a temper. Doors were slamming and plates were breaking. I even invited a friend to stay over but she couldn't hear anything. I think that they're just after me. I can see them appearing and disappearing in the hall. My boyfriend tries to be supportive but I know that he doesn't really understand because he can't see these people. Once I saw 'you're close to death' written in the condensation on the bathroom mirror but when I went back with my boyfriend the words had gone. I was terrified. Sometimes I just yell at them to leave me alone but they won't.

One of my friends said that she thinks that something

very evil is following me and doesn't want to let me go. I'm not supposed to talk to it but I can't help it. Whenever I see these people I'm always frightened and angry. They do sometimes disappear when I shout. I told my brother thinking he would understand but he said to tell a psychiatrist about it and get some pills to make them go away. I do take medication for depression and anxiety, but, I'm sure I'm not hallucinating because I know the dead people are really there.

Zena, 21

My friend Helen's mum does psychic readings from her home. One time she held a séance and allowed me and Helen to sit in on it. Everybody was sitting around a round table holding hands. The spirit of a young boy came through. He told us that he had been murdered when he was twelve years old by a man who was never caught. He also told us that his parents had been abusive and that his life had been unhappy. He wouldn't tell us his name or his parents' name and Helen's mum stopped the séance because she had a bad feeling about it.

After everybody had gone, Helen and I sat in the room talking and then decided to try to contact this spirit again by ourselves. We asked him to give us some physical sign of his presence. The light bulb went out and the papers on the coffee table fell onto the floor.

Because we had been making such a noise, Helen's

mum came out of her study to see what we were doing. She was so angry with us that Helen was grounded and I was banned from going to her house for two months.

I only saw Helen at school and she told me that she was finding it difficult to sleep at night because someone kept shaking her bed in the middle of the night.

Eventually, things calmed down. Perhaps the spirit moved on. Neither I nor Helen has ever tried to contact spirits again. The view I take is that if a spirit needs to get in touch with you they will be able to find a way.

Sam, 25

One thing I have learned in my life is that it is a bad idea to try to contact dead people. I tried once when I was a teenager and it was a horrible experience. I did actually hear voices but they were garbled and frightening. I didn't sleep properly for weeks afterwards.

It is something that teenagers do because they watch horror movies, read books about vampires or whatever and think it will be cool to have a séance or try some magic. Basically they dare each other and no one wants to seem like a coward.

I would say that there are some things that it is better to be a coward about. There are bad things out there and you don't want to bring yourselves to their attention.

Vanessa, 25

Not long after I first started college we decided to try channelling spirits at one of my friends' twenty-first birthday party. As we all sat in a circle and asked spirits to make themselves known to us I felt someone tickle my ribs. I looked behind me but there was no one there. Another friend felt something 'muss' her hair and we all began giggling. I then felt a gentle shove against my shoulder and for some reason shouted out 'Stop it Mark!'

The friend whose birthday it was stared at me open-mouthed. Her father had died of a cardiac arrest when she was seventeen. His name was Mark and he was known as a practical joker who always tickled and nudged her. We think it was the spirit of her father that came through to us on her birthday.

Roberta, 18

When we went on a school camping trip my friend Jessie and I brought along her mother's Ouija board. She didn't know that we took it or she would've been mad. We'd never played it before and so we didn't know whether it would work or not.

At midnight seven of us sat inside the camp hut and lit seven candles. My friend Gavin tried to speak to his dead grandfather. The glass began moving around the board but although it had pointed to 'yes' when Gavin had asked if it was his granddad, he wasn't so sure. He asked it what day his grandfather had died but it didn't give any answers, it just slid around on the board

We were confused and let go of the planchette, it kept spinning all by itself. I didn't want to touch it again but everyone insisted that we finish what we were doing so I joined in again. It spelled out EVIL. By this time, Gavin knew that it wasn't his grandfather's spirit we had called up.

I remember hearing that Ouija boards often open channels to evil entities if you don't know what you're doing with them. I said that I wanted to stop.

We didn't know what to do. Jessie told us that to stop the board bringing up spirits you had to turn it face down and tell the spirits that the session had ended, so that's what we did. Immediately the wind stopped and everything seemed very quiet. I would never touch one of those things again.

Kirsty, 23

I am surrounded by spirits every day. I can be walking down the street or in a store and spirits come and talk to me. I can feel how they passed away. I get chest pains from heart victims or localised pain when someone has died of some form of cancer. I have also felt someone being strangled.

Lately, however, I am being followed around by a very malevolent spirit who pushes me and pulls my hair when

I'm asleep. It makes the lights go out and sometimes when this happens I can't breathe. I can sometimes see a shadowy figure out of the corner of my eye and he says 'Leave', to me all the time.

Once as I was cutting vegetables for supper he whispered 'Ouch' in my ear and I cut my finger straight after that.

I find it uncomfortable to talk about these things. I don't think he can do me any serious harm, but it is not nice to feel that there are bad spirits around you.

Debbie, 20

My flat mate Sasha and I were bored one night and decided to try a séance in my room. There was just the two of us and we made a circle of lit candles and sat together in the middle of them. At first we were being silly and tried to summon up the spirits of people like Sigmund Freud or Winston Churchill. Obviously none of them responded but as we quietened down the atmosphere in the room seemed to change.

There were some weird noises and then a mirror fell off the wall followed by some framed photographs. I could hear knocking on the wall but Sasha said that she couldn't hear anything. Then someone breathed on the back of my neck. I immediately got up and put the light on and couldn't see anything, but with the light on the room felt calmer.

Since then however, I can't sleep without the light on in my room. If I try to sleep in the dark, I get an overwhelming feeling that someone is in the room with me. My bed sometimes seems to shake slightly at night too. Both Sasha and I are looking for another place to live. I wish we'd never done the séance.

Glen, 52

As it happens I used to work as a medium. I'm not sure I really believed in it to start with. I had the idea that I had been in touch some spirits but when I started doing the stage show it was all based on cold reading, lucky guesses and intuition. I am quite good at standing on a stage and keeping an audience entertained and I was able to improvise some interesting material.

As a general rule if you stand up there and tell an audience that someone's mother or grandmother is coming through, then you can see from their reactions who has lost someone recently. From there is a matter of trying to elicit some responses from them by making vague claims about what the spirit is saying.

I am making myself sound like a complete charlatan. But I started out doing this work because I genuinely did sometimes feel like I was in contact with spirits. It's just that you can't always count on a spirit contacting you when you are standing in front of an audience so you have to use a bit of stagecraft to make a show work.

I also did private readings. Sometimes these were no good – I couldn't feel anything about the client and had to resort to the tricks of the stage to make them feel I had told them something useful. It's quite shameful when someone is so grateful to receive a message from their loved ones and you know deep down that you have faked it.

I wouldn't be telling you all of these things if it wasn't for the fact I gave up this line of work five years ago. In the end it wasn't because I was ashamed. It was that I kept hearing this one particular spirit talking to me. Whoever I was trying to channel I would get this one voice coming through. It was a man who had died violently. I think in truth he was quite psychopathic. As a spirit he was extremely aggressive and irrational in his responses. I would hear him threatening me and making all kinds of abusive insults.

I would be on stage or in a private reading, and would open my mind to the spiritual realm in the hope of being able to contact a spirit who genuinely wanted to talk to the people I was with. But over and again this one abusive voice would come through.

In the end I decided that the only thing I could do was to give up. Mostly I only hear the voices when I open my mind up to them, and as long as I was trying to contact spirits I was going to keep being tormented by this one man.

I had a few nightmares after I gave up, and occasionally he would get through to me even though I didn't want him to. But in the end he drifted away and I haven't heard him now for several years. I am extremely happy not to hear that unpleasant voice ever again.

These days I run a coffee shop. It is hard work, but I feel happier than I did back when I was being a medium.